The Oliver Wight ABCD Checklist for Operational Excellence

The Oliver Wight ABCD Checklist for Operational Excellence

FIFTH EDITION

John Wiley & Sons, Inc.
New York · Chichester · Weinheim · Brisbane · Singapore · Toronto

This book is printed on acid-free paper. ∞

Copyright © 2000 by Oliver Wight International, Inc. All rights reserved.
Published by John Wiley & Sons, Inc.

Published simultaneously in Canada.

This publication is designed to provide accurate and authoritative information in regard to the subject matter covered. It is sold with the understanding that the publisher is not engaged in rendering legal, accounting, or other professional services. If legal advice or other expert assistance is required, the services of a competent professional person should be sought.

Library of Congress Cataloging-in-Publication Data:

The Oliver Wight ABCD checklist for operational excellence / Oliver Wight International, inc.—5th ed.
    p. cm.
    Originally published: 4th ed. Essex Juction, Vt. : Oliver Wight Publications, ©1993.
    Includes bibliographical references and index.
    ISBN 0-471-38819-X (pbk. : alk. paper)
    1. Industrial productivity—Measurement.   2. Strategic planning.   3. Total quality management.   4. Manufacturing resource planning.   5. Production control. I. Title: ABCD checklist for operational excellence. II. Wight, Oliver W. III. Oliver Wight International, inc.

HD56.25 .O38 2000
658.4′013—dc21
                                      00-033007
Printed in the United States of America.

10 9 8 7 6 5 4 3 2

ACKNOWLEDGMENTS

One person, or even a few people, did not author *The Oliver Wight ABCD Checklist for Operational Excellence.* It is a collection of the experiences of people from hundreds of companies compiled over a period of more than twenty-five years.

This fifth edition of the checklist is a revision of the fourth edition, built on the previous versions developed by Oliver Wight in the 1970s, a substantial revision to the checklist that was published in 1988, and a major revision that was published in 1993.

This edition of *The Oliver Wight ABCD Checklist* recognizes the rapid developments in management tools and techniques available to companies today. Its purpose is to expand the role of the checklist as an industry standard for operational performance measurement, thereby helping companies achieve world-class levels of performance.

- The development team for this checklist included:
- Luis Torres, who was the major contributor of the Strategic Planning chapter incorporating his knowledge of the subject matter
- Edna Talavera, who reviewed and updated the chapter on People/Team Processes
- Bill Boyst, who contributed to the update of the chapter on Total Quality and Continuous Improvement
- Tom Gillen, who provided the revision of the New Product Development chapter

- John Proud, who did a thorough review and update of the Planning and Control chapter

Special thanks are given to Jon Minerich and Jim Correll for the final editing of this book.

Sincere thanks go to the many Oliver Wight associates who participated and contributed ideas that were utilized in this revision. Our thanks to Jill Losik for all her support in making this effort possible. Together we have compiled a set of criteria that a company can use to determine how well it's operating, identify opportunities for improvement, and monitor its progress on the continuous journey to operational excellence.

I want to take this opportunity to thank the Oliver Wight International Board of Directors for asking me to coordinate this project. It has, indeed, been a pleasure to work with my associates in order to provide this guide for the benefit of all the companies in the world that will use it.

Jose M. Calderon
Oliver Wight International

CONTENTS

INTRODUCTION

Perspective

Are we doing the right things? How well are we doing them? Are we on the right track to world-class performance? Are we integrating people, processes, and tools? It is hard to imagine any more valuable questions than these for all managers to ask frequently. The answers reflect current levels of performance and reveal significant opportunities for improvement.

Finding the right answers, however, requires many more questions. This checklist raises those questions. As such, it is an important tool in appraising a company's effectiveness in developing the right processes to utilize the many technologies available to manufacturing companies today

A good checklist does more than tell you where you are today—it helps managers focus, align, and engage in what is required to become more competitive and achieve world-class levels of performance. Regular use of the checklist generates a consistent means of assessing progress. In addition, it identifies problems early, which allows the correction process to start immediately. Further, by comparing performance against established best practices, people are motivated to work in a more effective manner.

The Fifth Edition of the Oliver Wight ABCD Checklist

This new checklist is significantly more comprehensive than its predecessors. It kept the same organization of chapters but has a more in-

1

depth review. Our purpose was to simplify all the areas, keeping the book up to date with the latest evolutions and maintaining its status as the leading-edge checklist for operational excellence.

It would be an overwhelming task for most companies to attack, simultaneously, all of these business processes and their underlying technologies. Implementing all of these major changes at the same time would call for too much work to be done by people who already have full-time jobs of running the business.

There are significant risks in trying to do too much at one time: nothing gets done well, people burn out, and the competitive advantage is lost.

The chapter organization of this checklist allows a company to choose one of several of these basic business processes and concentrate its energies on that choice. The selection should be made based on the competitive priorities facing the business.

Qualitative Characteristics and Overview Items

Each chapter begins with brief qualitative characteristics of the various levels of performance—Class A, B, C, and D—for the processes in question. Then the overview items are listed including an executive summary. They're designed to allow executives to evaluate whether necessary processes exist and, if so, how well they are being used.

Detail Items

Following this executive summary, the Detail Items are identified and grouped under their respective Overview Items. These Detail Items provide additional information, guidance, the means for assessment, and make up the main body of the checklist. They're designed to provide operating managers with a tool for assessing the significant characteristics of each process, checking the vital "how to's" of each process, and analyzing in greater detail how well the processes are being used. For most of the Overview Items, numerous Detail Items are listed that will help determine your position on the scale for each overview item. A few

Overview Items, however, have no Detail Items, and these are noted in the text with an asterisk (*).

Duplication of Entries

This checklist covers multiple technologies and processes, and there is sometimes an overlap from one to another. For example, many of the Overview and Detail Items involved in effective People/Team processes are necessary for Total Quality/Continuous Improvement processes. Therefore, in some cases, it's been necessary to include the same items in more than one chapter. These have been noted in the text with a dagger(†).

Scoring of Responses

In the first three editions of the checklist, responses were limited to "yes" or "no" (or, where appropriate, "not applicable").

This new checklist maintains the fourth edition's scoring format, which enables responses to be made on a scale of 0 (Not Doing) to 4 (Excellent). This helps in identifying what's been done and what remains to be done, and can serve as an impetus for continuous improvement.

Objective

Our objective in publishing *The Oliver Wight Class ABCD Checklist for Operational Excellence* is to help companies become the best they can be. We hope you find this tool helps you to ask the right questions and determine the right answers to achieve absolute world-class performance, to become truly excellent in all operational aspects of the business. If so, then we have indeed produced a Class A product.

> Jim Correll
> Co-Chair
> Oliver Wight International

HOW TO USE THE CHECKLIST

Scoring the Results

The responses to both Overview and Detail Items are scored on a range from "Excellent" to "Not Doing," with three intermediate points. To determine where your performance falls on the range, use the following table as a guide.

Excellent
4 points
Highest expected level of results from performing this activity.

Very Good
3 points
Fully performing this activity and has achieved original goals associated with it.

Fair
2 points
Have most of the processes, and tools are in place, but not fully utilizing the process and/or not getting the desired results.

Poor
1 point
People, processes, and tools are not at the minimum prescribed level, resulting in little, if any, benefit.

Not Doing
0 points
This activity is required but currently not being performed.

This method of scoring was chosen for the following reasons: it recognizes the work people have done, even though the company may not yet be at the "Excellent" level; it indicates where, and how much, additional work is required to achieve Class A results; it provides a means for continuous improvement—even at the Class A level, there is still room for improvement.

Most people answer the detail questions first, then use this information as a guide for answering the overview questions.

It's important to point out that the score for the overview questions is not an average of the scores for the detail questions. The detail questions are designed to help in determining the score for the overview questions, but not all questions are of equal importance.

Calculating the Letter Grade

Once the Overview Items have been answered, complete the process of determining the letter grade for the chapter by averaging the numerical scores for the Overview Items.

- Average greater than 3.5 means that you are at the Class A level for that set of business processes.
- Average between 2.5 and 3.49 qualifies for Class B level.
- Average between 1.5 and 2.49 means a Class C level.
- Average less than 1.5 indicates a Class D level.

Moreover, before any company can be rated with confidence, there should be *at least three months of sustained performance.* As we all know, there are periods when everything appears to be working well, but it does not necessarily mean that the company has implemented the right set of tools or has learned to manage effectively using them. A single point in time is not sufficient to arrive at a firm conclusion.

Even a Class A rating in a particular set of business processes, however, should not be interpreted as achieving full utilization of your potential. A company achieving a Class A level of performance can still get better.

For example, if the company has achieved a Class A level of excellence in New Product Development Processes, there are obviously other business functions in which Class A can be attained. In addition, achieving Class A in New Product Development Processes doesn't mean there is no room for improvement, even in that area.

Many companies take pride in attaining a Class A level and then use this accomplishment as inspiration for further improvements. In fact, all of the companies who have attained the Class A level of performance tend to be very self-critical. They continue to see what remains, what can be done, and are aggressively pushing forward.

"I know we can get a lot better and must."

"The competition is tough, but so are we."

"The emphasis in our business is to give the customer what he wants, when he wants it, with continually lower lead times and excellent quality."

These are quotes from companies that are remarkably good today, but will be even better tomorrow.

Performance Improvement Process

The best way to use the checklist is as a vision of what could exist in your company, and pursue it aggressively, systematically, and relent-lessly. Companies using the checklist in this way are using it effectively, and are achieving the potential of their organizations.

Not all companies use the Oliver Wight ABCD Checklist this way. Some companies use the checklist merely as a results indicator in the later stages of an implementation program. While beneficial, this does little to ensure continuous improvement.

For this reason, we recommend following the steps listed below to enable your company to use the checklist to achieve better results both in the short term and on a sustained basis in the future.

Performance Improvement Steps

1. Assess current status
2. Determine the gaps and prioritize based on competitive advantage
3. Tailor the checklist to your company's immediate needs
4. Develop action plans
5. Measure progress through monthly management reviews
6. Conduct monthly management reviews

1. Assess Current Status

The performance improvement process begins with an assessment of the company's current strengths and weaknesses against the Oliver

Wight ABCD Checklist. Many companies start by answering the questions that pertain to their areas of focus. If planning and control processes are where your company can gain the greatest competitive advantage the quickest, then you might focus only on this chapter. On the other hand, you may choose to address all five chapters to get an overall assessment of the situation in your company. You can then use the entire checklist to determine and prioritize those areas where you want to focus.

Most companies meet in groups of ten to twenty people to discuss the questions in the checklist. The groups should be made of customers and suppliers to the process (either internal and/or external), which allows for discussion and the comparing of differences. For example, if one person feels the master schedule is well managed but others feel it has been managed poorly, then a healthy discussion will take place. It's important to have several levels of management take part in these discussions, because it's typical for things to look better when viewed from the top of the organization.

There are a few prerequisites for these discussions to be useful. The first is that the participants must be knowledgeable. This means being familiar with the terms and techniques that are referenced and having an adequate understanding as to why the processes are important for the company to operate at a very high standard.

Second is the assumption that the answers will come from people of "good intentions." Knowledgeable people who are sincerely attempting to be objective can avoid seeing the world through rose-colored glasses or being overly critical to the extent that any minor imperfection leads to a negative response.

No matter how well phrased the items in this checklist may be, we recognize that degrees of interpretation are required to answer them. We also realize that a significant element of judgment is needed before answering many items. The combination of interpretation and judgment will, hopefully, lead to healthy internal discussion. Often companies elect to use knowledgeable outsiders to facilitate the process to ensure an accurate Class A assessment. The checklist will be productive if companies use it to review why these processes are important, what each process consists of, how the process can contribute to improvements, and how to accomplish these improvements.

2. Determine the Gaps and Prioritize Based on Competitive Advantage

Once the assessment has been completed, it is a relatively simple process to identify the gaps. The difference between the score on any particular statement and 4.0 is the gap between your company and the best practices identified in the checklist. The more difficult job is to determine the priority. One way to determine the priority is to simply to look at the gap in the scores and focus on the statements that have the biggest gap. A second method is to determine which gaps are the easiest to fix; a third is to determine what the benefit to the company would be if you closed the gap on a particular statement. The best approach is to take into consideration all three when ranking the priorities. This last approach takes some time and effort but does provide a more organized approach that will give you the best results.

We can't emphasize enough the importance of doing a cost/benefit analysis. The real intention is to make dramatic improvements in the company's competitive position. A change in senior management or changes in the economic conditions often turn Class A into the "flavor of the month" and progress comes to a quick halt without a good bottom line analysis.

3. Tailor Checklist to Your Company's Immediate Needs

The Oliver Wight Checklist was created to apply to all companies; therefore, we used generic terms. However, many companies have adopted specific terms that people are familiar with. Companies also have organizational structures that may be different from the ones implied in the checklist. General Manager is a good example. We have implied that a General Manager has all functions (e.g. sales, marketing, manufacturing, engineering, finance, etc.) reporting to that position. That is not the case in many companies. To help the people in the company understand the checklist, we strongly suggest you rewrite the checklist to make it fit your company's terminology and structure. You must be very careful, however, not to change the intent of the question. Many times, in helping companies with their Class A journey, we encounter significant resistance, which is to be expected when asking people to make major changes to their processes and behaviors. A common response we have heard is, "Change the question because we don't do things that way at our company." Rather than changing the question, we should focus on improving the current business process.

Tailoring the checklist also allows a company to reorganize the questions to fit their implementation activities, create a subset of the checklist containing the items being actively worked on, and focus attention on these items. This is a big help when trying to manage a large project, which Class A often turns into when the benefits are properly documented and understood.

4. Develop Action Plans

The next critically important step is to establish the action plans to fill the gaps and achieve the results identified in the cost/benefit analysis. These action plans lead to accountabilities for the areas that need improvement. Someone (or several people) would be assigned responsibility for meeting the action plans in the planned time frame for each task in the action plan.

To prevent backsliding in areas where the assessment has shown good results, one person (or several people) would be assigned accountability for maintaining the current level of performance on each of these items.

5. Measure Progress

As progress is made, it should be recorded against the action plans created. Some questions can be measured quantitatively. For example, bill of material accuracy can be plotted, showing progress from the starting point to the agreed-upon goal. Other questions are more subjective, but still capable of measurement. An example would be surveying people's perceptions on top management's commitment to quality.

6. Conduct Monthly Management Reviews

Experience has shown it's important to conduct monthly reviews of the measurements. The purpose is to monitor progress on currently active items and watch for slippage on established items. As with any implementation management review, the questions to ask are:

- Have the milestones been achieved?
- If not, what can be done to bring this aspect of the implementation back on schedule?
- What issues need to be resolved to continue our progress?

With these steps in mind as a method for improving the operational excellence of your organization, let's now look at the five chapters of the Oliver Wight ABCD Checklist.

1
STRATEGIC PLANNING PROCESSES

QUALITATIVE CHARACTERISTICS

Class A   Strategic planning is an ongoing process and carries an intense customer/community, shareholder, and employee focus. The strategic planning process provides direction to all elements of the company and drives decisions and actions. Employees at all levels can articulate and share the company's vision and its overall strategic direction. They can also articulate their roles in the implementation and execution of the strategic plan.

Class B   A formal process, performed by line executives and managers at least once per year. Major decisions are tested first against the strategic plan. The company's vision statement is widely shared.

Class C   Strategic planning is done infrequently, but provides some direction to how the business is run.

Class D   Strategic planning is nonexistent or totally removed from driving customer, shareholder, and employee satisfaction.

OVERVIEW ITEMS

1-1 COMMITMENT TO EXCELLENCE

The company has an obsession with excellence and is not satisfied with the status quo. Executives provide the leadership necessary for change. They articulate the motivations for positive change and communicate them throughout the organization—by actions as well as words.

1-2 LEADERSHIP TEAM

The organization has a leadership team consisting of key executives who recognize they must sponsor and guide the members of the organization by taking a forward position and acting on key issues.

1-3 VISION AND MISSION

Vision and mission statements for the organization exist. The vision statement focuses on the future of the business and shows employees, shareholders, and customers what the company wants to become. The mission statement outlines the purpose and nature of the business and reinforces the reason for its existence; These items include statements on products and/or services, customers, community, and employees. They are a broad road map of where the company wants to be in the future and do not contain specific operational or financial measurements.

1-4 BUSINESS PERFORMANCE ASSESSMENT

A process exists that assesses the company's business performance in the four areas of success (measures of success): customer satisfaction, shareholder/stakeholder satisfaction, employee satisfaction, and community satisfaction.

1-5 ANALYSIS OF EXTERNAL ENVIRONMENT AND INTERNAL CAPABILITIES

Assessment processes, using facts and data, exist to determine how well the organization is performing with respect to all of the key drivers within the measures of success.

1-6 CASE FOR CHANGE

When the assessment of business performance indicates the existence of threats, opportunities, and/or the necessity for improvement, a case for change is presented to all employees of the company.

1-7 STRATEGY CREATION

The strategic planning process is initiated by Top Management and represents input from key people throughout the organization. Each and every strategy is documented and is linked to and supports the strategic goals.

1-8 ESTABLISHING STRATEGIC GOALS

Strategic goals are recognized as ends to which efforts are to be directed. Strategic goals require significant changes in the way in which the business operates and may take several years to implement.

1-9 PEOPLE AND COMMUNICATIONS

It is recognized that the successful implementation of strategies is a direct function of people involvement and continuous communication.

1-10 BUSINESS PLAN INTEGRATION

All goals and strategies are integrated into the business plan, which is used to develop and communicate annual financial plans that incorporate input from all operating departments of the company.

1-11 GOAL DEPLOYMENT AND IMPLEMENTATION
A process exists whereby the strategies and goals are deployed throughout the organization to gain focus, alignment and engagement throughout the company.

1-12 MEASURE RESULTS
It is recognized that strategic goals and strategies are deployed from management throughout the organization and that results are reported from the organization to management. A process exists to monitor progress against plans and to take corrective action when needed.

1-13 DIAGNOSIS AND REVIEW
Systematic reviews are done throughout the year to determine how annual goals are being achieved. These reviews include: methods employed, study of data, and comparison of plans against activities and plans against results.

1-14 REFLECTION
Executive management, individually or as a group, dedicates time to reassess the logic of their strategies and related goals and their achievements.

1-15 ONGOING, FORMAL GOAL SETTING AND STRATEGIC PLANNING
Goal setting and strategic planning are part of a formal process in which all executive managers have active, visible leadership roles.

1-16 EDUCATION AND TRAINING†
Education and training is viewed as a strategic advantage and the knowledge gained is measured by successful application on the job.

OVERVIEW AND DETAIL ITEMS

4—EXCELLENT
3—VERY GOOD
2—FAIR
1—POOR
0—NOT DOING

1-1 COMMITMENT TO EXCELLENCE

☐ ☐ ☐ ☐ ☐

The company has an obsession with excellence and is not satisfied with the status quo. Executives provide the leadership necessary for change. They articulate the motivations for positive change and communicate them throughout the organization— by actions as well as words.

1-1a   Commitment is demonstrated by the actions that the company is taking at all levels to achieve excellence. Communication and allocation of resources—time, people, and money—support the actions.

☐ ☐ ☐ ☐ ☐

1-1b   Management is committed to learn from the people they serve in order to provide unparalleled quality products and services.

☐ ☐ ☐ ☐ ☐

1-2 LEADERSHIP TEAM

☐ ☐ ☐ ☐ ☐

The organization has a leadership team consisting of key executives who recognize they must sponsor and guide the members of the organization by taking a forward position and acting on key issues.

1-2a   Each member of the leadership team is committed to and involved in improving the way the business is run.

☐ ☐ ☐ ☐ ☐

1-2b   The leadership team is focused on the direction of improving customer, shareholder, and employee satisfaction. The direction is consistent and constant.

☐ ☐ ☐ ☐ ☐

4—EXCELLENT 3—VERY GOOD 2—FAIR 1—POOR 0—NOT DOING

1-2c   The leadership team is committed to education for themselves and the rest of the organization.
☐ ☐ ☐ ☐ ☐

1-3 VISION AND MISSION
☐ ☐ ☐ ☐ ☐

Vision and mission statements for the organization exist. The vision statement focuses on the future of the business and shows employees, shareholders, and customers what the company wants to become. The mission statement outlines the purpose and nature of the business and reinforces the reason for its existence; these items include statements on products and/or services, customers, community, and employees. They are a broad road map of where the company wants to be in the future and do not contain specific operational or financial measurements.

1-3a   The vision and mission statements are leader—initiated and are shared and supported by all the members of the organization.
☐ ☐ ☐ ☐ ☐

1-3b   The vision is positive and inspiring. It is tested against the values of the company to support core beliefs, desired corporate structure, and standards of behavior.
☐ ☐ ☐ ☐ ☐

1-3c   The mission is clear and concise, and provides information as to the nature and existence of the business, its products and services, and the value they provide to the customers and/or society.
☐ ☐ ☐ ☐ ☐

4—EXCELLENT
3—VERY GOOD
2—FAIR
1—POOR
0—NOT DOING

☐ ☐ ☐ ☐ ☐

1-4 BUSINESS PERFORMANCE ASSESSMENT

A process exists that assesses the company's business performance in the four areas of success (measures of success): customer satisfaction, shareholder/stakeholder satisfaction, employee satisfaction, and community satisfaction.

1-4a   Key drivers are identified within the cus-   ☐ ☐ ☐ ☐ ☐
tomer satisfaction measures of success.
They may include, but are not limited to,
product fitness for use, price/cost, service,
delivery, quality, brand recognition, and
personal relationships.

1-4b   Key drivers are identified within the share-   ☐ ☐ ☐ ☐ ☐
holder satisfaction measures of success.
They may include, but are not limited to,
profit, growth, market share, cash flow, div-
idends, stock price, return on assets, economic value added, and corporate image.

1-4c   Key drivers arc identified within the em-   ☐ ☐ ☐ ☐ ☐
ployee satisfaction measures of success.
They may include, but are not limited to,
pay, benefits, opportunities, job security,
pride in work, pride in company, openness,
fairness, friendliness, teamwork, cama-
raderie, and innovation.

4—EXCELLENT 3—VERY GOOD 2—FAIR 1—POOR 0—NOT DOING

1-4d   Key drivers are identified within the community satisfaction measures of success. They may include, but are not limited to, environmental protection, civic responsibility, stable employment, facility appearance, traffic flow, and other activities that make the company a responsible community member.

☐ ☐ ☐ ☐ ☐

1-5 ANALYSIS OF EXTERNAL ENVIRONMENT AND INTERNAL CAPABILITIES

☐ ☐ ☐ ☐ ☐

Assessment processes, using facts and data, exist to determine how well the organization is performing with respect to all of the key drivers within the measures of success.

External Environment

A strengths, weaknesses, opportunities, and threats analysis and customer needs analysis of the external environment, including customers, competitors, suppliers, shareholders, technology, government, and community, are made to determine the present level of performance, satisfaction, and current conditions with respect to the key measures of success.

1-5a   In assessing customer satisfaction, there is a methodology that clearly hears the "voice of the customer." The customers' voices are quantified and documented against the key drivers. This assessment is compared to the customers' perceptions of the competitions' performance in each respective market for products and services. Customer needs and expectations are also documented and included within this assessment.

1-5b   In assessing shareholder satisfaction, a methodology exists that clearly determines their satisfaction. Shareholder satisfaction is quantified and documented against the key drivers. Shareholder expectations are also documented and included within this assessment.

1-5c   The company continuously measures its operational excellence by benchmarking products, services, and practices against the toughest competitors within and outside of the industry. This information is used to identify "best practices" and establish performance benchmarks. Also, an analysis of the internal capabilities is made, with particular attention to the company's infrastructure and its workforce capability to execute, compete, and accommodate change.

4—EXCELLENT
3—VERY GOOD
2—FAIR
1—POOR
0—NOT DOING

1-5d   In assessing employee satisfaction, a methodology exists that clearly determines their level of commitment and the organizational climate. Employee satisfaction is quantified and documented against the key drivers. Employee expectations are also documented and included within this assessment.

☐ ☐ ☐ ☐ ☐

Internal Capabilities

The assessment of internal capabilities includes an evaluation of the key company processes and how well they are integrated.

1-5e   This assessment examines the ability of processes such as strategic planning, planning and control, new product development and introduction, total quality and continuous improvement, supplier capabilities and performance, people, teamwork, and organizational performance.

☐ ☐ ☐ ☐ ☐

1-5f   This assessment includes consideration of existing and future financial resources and core competencies.

☐ ☐ ☐ ☐ ☐

1-6 CASE FOR CHANGE
When the assessment of business performance indicates the existence of threats, opportunities and/or the necessity for improvement, a case for change is presented to all employees of the company.

☐ ☐ ☐ ☐ ☐

4—EXCELLENT 3—VERY GOOD 2—FAIR 1—POOR 0—NOT DOING

1-6a   The case for change flows from the vision and the key measures of success. ☐ ☐ ☐ ☐ ☐

1-6b   The case for change is a compelling argument explaining the importance for change, what happens if change does not occur, and how the customers, shareholders, and employees will benefit from the change. ☐ ☐ ☐ ☐ ☐

1-6c   The case for change is continuously communicated by the leadership team. ☐ ☐ ☐ ☐ ☐

1-7 STRATEGY CREATION

☐ ☐ ☐ ☐ ☐

The strategic planning process is initiated by Top Management and represents input from key people throughout the organization. Each and every strategy is documented and is linked to and supports the strategic goals.

1-7a   A method exists to create potential strategies based on the results of the external environment and of internal capabilities analyses, guided heavily by the principle of sustainable competitive advantage. ☐ ☐ ☐ ☐ ☐

1-7b   A method exists to clarify and combine similar strategies and to prioritize and select the strategies to be implemented. ☐ ☐ ☐ ☐ ☐

1-7c   Selected strategies are tested against the company's vision, performance measures, and each other for congruence and/or conflict. These strategies represent the road-map toward the achievement of the vision and provide adequate direction for all areas of the business.

□ □ □ □ □

1-8 ESTABLISHING STRATEGIC GOALS

□ □ □ □ □

Strategic goals are recognized as ends to which efforts are to be directed. Strategic goals require significant changes in the way in which the business operates and may take several years to implement.

1-8a   Strategic goals are established to overcome competitors' advantages or to extend the company's competitive position and exploit new opportunities.

□ □ □ □ □

1-8b   Strategic goals are stretch in nature, attainable, measurable, agreed upon, relevant, and time bound.

□ □ □ □ □

1-9 PEOPLE AND COMMUNICATIONS

□ □ □ □ □

It is recognized that the successful implementation of strategies is a direct function of people involvement and continuous communication.

1-9a   The goals and strategies are executed by people within the dominant structure of the organization, not by an outside team, and responsibility for implementation is clearly defined.

□ □ □ □ □

	4—EXCELLENT	3—VERY GOOD	2—FAIR	1—POOR	0—NOT DOING

1-9b   Leadership concentrates on important/ non-urgent items.

1-9c   It is recognized that education, training, and communication are management's most leveraged activities.

1-9d   Communication flows from management throughout the organization and from the organization to management.

1-9e   The customer/supplier relationship for every employee's process is the foundation for education and training.

1-10 BUSINESS PLAN INTEGRATION

All goals and strategies are integrated into the business plan which is used to develop and communicate annual financial plans that incorporate input from all operating departments of the company.

1-10a   The company has a business plan which covers market share and projections, financial performance, new product development, customer service levels, resources, and desired inventory levels. The business plan is used in the Sales and Operating Planning (S&OP) process.

4—EXCELLENT 3—VERY GOOD 2—FAIR 1—POOR 0—NOT DOING

1-10b   Goals and strategies and their respective measures of success, which were developed from the strategic planning process, are documented and integrated into the business plan.

☐ ☐ ☐ ☐ ☐

1-10c   All annual financial plans are congruent with the business strategies and include detailed financial information by department.

☐ ☐ ☐ ☐ ☐

1-10d   Resources required to support the strategies and goals are quantified and time-phased into the business plan.

☐ ☐ ☐ ☐ ☐

1-10e   Action plans required to implement the strategic goals and performance against these plans is reviewed quarterly and documented as part of the business planning and review process.

☐ ☐ ☐ ☐ ☐

1-10f   Corrective action plans are developed to keep goal achievement on track and include a mechanism to ensure that sales and operations plans are synchronized with the business plan.

☐ ☐ ☐ ☐ ☐

1-11 GOAL DEPLOYMENT AND IMPLEMENTATION

☐ ☐ ☐ ☐ ☐

A process exists whereby the goals and strategies are deployed throughout the organization to gain focus, alignment and engagement throughout the company.

	4—EXCELLENT	3—VERY GOOD	2—FAIR	1—POOR	0—NOT DOING

1-11a Barriers to change are recognized, addressed, and resolved.

1-11b Objectives are systematically deployed through "sponsors" to the appropriate people in the organization, who have responsibility to contribute to the achievement of the goal(s).

1-11c At every point in the organization where a strategic goal is deployed, detailed strategies and action plans are developed and documented to support the strategic goals.

1-11d People at all levels who will implement the strategies and plans have a sense of ownership and are committed to success.

1-12 MEASURE RESULTS

It is recognized that strategic goals and strategies are deployed from management throughout the organization and that results are reported from the organization to management. A process exists to monitor progress against plans and to take corrective action when needed.

1-12a Executive management focuses a sufficient amount of their time on ensuring that breakthrough strategic goals are being achieved.

1-12b A process exists which measures and reports results, including roadblocks and problems.

4—EXCELLENT
3—VERY GOOD
2—FAIR
1—POOR
0—NOT DOING

1-13 DIAGNOSIS AND REVIEW

☐ ☐ ☐ ☐ ☐

Systematic reviews are done throughout the year to determine how annual goals are being achieved. These reviews include: methods employed, study of data, and comparison of plans against activities and plans against results.

1-13a   Executive management exhibits leadership in goal deployment by selecting key goals and/or strategies and physically walking through their implementation from the top of the organization to the bottom. They pay particular attention to employee understanding, performance to plan, root cause of problems, and commitment.

☐ ☐ ☐ ☐ ☐

1-13b   Monthly formal review sessions of the critical goals and strategies are conducted in order to create awareness and commitment throughout the organization.

☐ ☐ ☐ ☐ ☐

1-14 REFLECTION

☐ ☐ ☐ ☐ ☐

Executive management, individually or as a group, dedicates time to reassess the logic of their strategies and related goals and their achievements.

1-14a   Executive management assesses their progress against key drivers within the measures of success over time.

☐ ☐ ☐ ☐ ☐

1-14b   Progress, or lack of progress, stimulates executive management to reinforce, maintain, alter, or delete specific goals or strategies.

☐ ☐ ☐ ☐ ☐

1-15 ONGOING, FORMAL GOAL SETTING AND STRATEGIC PLANNING

Goal setting and strategic planning are part of a formal process in which all executive managers have active, visible leadership roles.

1-15a   The goals and strategies are reviewed at least quarterly (more frequently if necessary), and executive management, as a group, reviews progress on all major development and improvement initiatives at least monthly.

1-15b   The review process uses a systematic method to document, analyze, and incorporate revisions into the business plan.

1-16 EDUCATION AND TRAINING

Education and training is viewed as a strategic advantage and the knowledge gained is measured by successful application on the job.

1-16a   Management views education and training as a strategic advantage, and their attitude and actions demonstrate commitment and involvement to educate and train all necessary people fully prior to the implementation of new processes and tools/ technologies.

1-16b   Education and training are aligned with the strategic initiatives to assure the right education and training is done and it is cost effective.

4—EXCELLENT 3—VERY GOOD 2—FAIR 1—POOR 0—NOT DOING

1-16c   The education and training program recognizes people at all levels as experts in
their respective areas. The education program uses these people to communicate
company goals and objectives, facilitate
the required change process, and measure
performance results.

1-16d   The education and training approach is
based on the principles of process and
people behavior change in an organization
rather than merely on fact-transfer regarding specific tools or technologies.

1-16e   Employee performance evaluations are
tied to successful application of the knowledge gained in the education and training
sessions.

1-16f   The company has committed adequate resources, time, and finances to education
and training.

2
PEOPLE/TEAM PROCESSES

QUALITATIVE CHARACTERISTICS

Class A   Trust, teamwork, mutual respect, open communications, and a high degree of employment security are hallmarks of the employee/company relationship. A formalized team structure is evident throughout the organization. Employees are very pleased with the company and proud to be part of it.

Class B   Employees have confidence in the company's management and consider the company a good place to work. Effective use is being made of small work groups throughout the organization.

Class C   Traditional employment practices are largely being used. Management considers the company's people to be an important, but not vital, resource of the business. Use of small work groups is evident in some areas of the organization.

Class D   The employee/employer relationship is neutral at best; sometimes negative.

OVERVIEW ITEMS

2-1 COMMITMENT TO EXCELLENCE
All levels of management have a commitment to treating people with trust, openness, and honesty. Teams are used to multiply the strength of the organization. People are empowered to take direct action, make decisions, and initiate changes.

2-2 CULTURE
A comprehensive culture exists to support and enhance effective people and team processes.

2-3 TRUST
Openness, honesty, and constructive feedback are highly valued and demonstrated organizational traits. All employees are treated consistently and rewarded based on contributions to the business goal, regardless of function and/or job level.

2-4 TEAMWORK†
Clearly identifiable teams are utilized as the primary means to direct, organize, and perform the work, as opposed to individual job functions or independent work stations.

2-5 EMPLOYMENT CONTINUITY AND DEVELOPMENT†
Employment continuity is important to the company, as long as the employee exceeds the minimum acceptable job requirements, and the level of business makes it viable.

2-6 EDUCATION AND TRAINING†
An active education and training program focused on business issues, customer issues, and operational improvements is in place for all com-

pany personnel. Its objectives include enhancing people's skills, increasing process flexibility, sharing tools/technology understanding, and meeting future needs. Education and training are viewed as a strategic advantage, and the knowledge gained is measured by its successful application to the job.

2-7 WORK DESIGN†
Jobs are designed to reinforce the company goal of a team-based, empowered workforce.

2-8 CONGRUENCE
People policies, organizational development, and education and training are consistent with the company vision, mission, and business strategies.

OVERVIEW AND DETAIL ITEMS

4—EXCELLENT 3—VERY GOOD 2—FAIR 1—POOR 0—NOT DOING

2-1 COMMITMENT TO EXCELLENCE
All levels of management have a commitment to treating people with trust, openness, and honesty. Teams are used to multiply the strength of the organization. People are empowered to take direct action, make decisions, and initiate changes.

2-1a   Top management demonstrates a strong commitment to teamwork and has a clear understanding of the concepts of group dynamics and group process.

2-1b   There is a clearly established policy to foster and reinforce teamwork throughout the organization.

2-1c   There is an "open door" policy evident throughout the different management levels within the organization.

2-1d   Team activities, resources requirements, and follow-up tasks are included as integral parts of the company's business plan deployment.

2-2 CULTURE
A comprehensive culture exists to support and enhance effective people and team processes.

2-2a   Employees are empowered to take direct action whenever they encounter a problem that is likely to impact customer satisfaction, product or service quality, cost, and/or schedule.

2-2b   Operating decisions are made at the lowest possible level, flowing logically and expeditiously throughout the organization.

2-2c   There are few "status" distinctions between managers and workers. There is a clear intention to minimize artificial barriers that would be detrimental to creating an open, highly empowered work environment.

2-2d   Information-passing processes, such as team meetings and "state-of-the-business" assemblies, are a regular part of work.

4—EXCELLENT   3—VERY GOOD   2—FAIR   1—POOR   0—NOT DOING

2-2e   A process is in place to help workers expand their roles to become team players; (highly skilled, knowledge resources, customer advocates, trainers, problem solvers, and decision makers). This process includes training and follow-up support.

☐ ☐ ☐ ☐ ☐

2-2f   A process is in place to help supervisors, managers, and technical support professionals modify and expand their roles to become coaches, facilitators, customer advocates, barrier busters, motivators, and leaders. This process includes training and follow-up support.

☐ ☐ ☐ ☐ ☐

2-2g   Major achievements stemming from the continuous improvement and empowerment efforts are formally recognized and rewarded.

☐ ☐ ☐ ☐ ☐

2-2h   Major improvements and lessons learned are documented and integrated into daily management processes and future organizational development plans.

☐ ☐ ☐ ☐ ☐

2-3 TRUST
Openness, honesty, and constructive feedback are highly valued and demonstrated organizational traits. All employees are treated consistently and rewarded based on contributions to the business goals, regardless of function and/or job level.

☐ ☐ ☐ ☐ ☐

4—EXCELLENT   3—VERY GOOD   2—FAIR   1—POOR   0—NOT DOING

2-3a   Continuously improving communication between management and workers is emphasized and practiced as a routine task.

2-3b   The information flow is adequate and timely enough for people at all levels to understand the current performance of the business (e.g., customers, competition, strategies, profitability) and effectively utilize operational data (e.g., quality, service level, schedule, etc.) for problem identification, resolution, and improvement recommendations.

2-3c   Management and employees regularly provide customer/supplier feedback and setup opportunities for direct, face-to-face meetings between team members and customers/suppliers. These communication linkages are regularly used to identify customer needs, leading to process and product improvements.

2-3d   A mechanism exists for manager and peer feedback to occur on a routine basis. Managers also receive regular feedback from the people they manage.

4—EXCELLENT   3—VERY GOOD   2—FAIR   1—POOR   0—NOT DOING

2-3e   A performance-management system has ☐ ☐ ☐ ☐ ☐
been established to provide employee feedback and consistency in salary compensation based on key performance indicators
that are directly linked to the company's
business plan, strategies, and goals, and to
the performance of business processes.

2-4 TEAMWORK†   ☐ ☐ ☐ ☐ ☐

Clearly identifiable teams are utilized as the
primary means to direct, organize, and perform the
work, as opposed to individual job functions or
independent work stations.

2-4a   There is a team management structure ☐ ☐ ☐ ☐ ☐
which clearly defines roles, responsibilities, and functionality of the different
types of teams:

- *Lead teams (management teams)* include
top and middle managers whose main
responsibility is to provide clear direction, focus, and follow-up to inter-
functional project team activities that
are directly linked to corporate strategies
and goals.
- *Project teams (inter-functional teams)*
include technical and professional personnel who have been specifically selected by management teams for their
expertise on the subject matter at hand.
This team's main responsibility is to

work on specifically assigned inter-functional projects that are directly linked to corporate strategies and goals.

- *Process teams* are mainly cross-functional teams that support and operate the processes of the business. They concentrate their efforts on main processes that cross the entire business, shortening the gap between customer and suppliers, so that information, goods, and services flow quickly throughout the supply chain. Process teams work to improve the performance of the whole process, as opposed to the optimization of departmental functional performance.

2-4b   All team members, managers, supervisors, and technical and support people have been formally introduced to the concepts of high-performance work teams through company education programs.   □ □ □ □ □

2-4c   The roles/jobs have been formally structured to support the work team approach.   □ □ □ □ □

2-4d   Teams have clear direction and complete understanding of their mission, scopes, responsibilities, and operating guidelines.   □ □ □ □ □

2-4e   Teams meet on a regularly-scheduled basis and/or on an as-needed basis to solve problems and explore opportunities in their respective areas of responsibility.   □ □ □ □ □

2-4f   Teams and the functions they perform are almost entirely self-contained and managed by the group itself. Group members rely on one another for cross training, problem solving, handling of administrative duties, and mutual support.

2-4g   Teams use a structured and efficient problem-solving methodology to analyze, improve, and control the work flow and processes in order to improve the effectiveness of the operation.

2-4h   Teams have a defined process for gaining direct feedback from both external and internal customers.

2-4i   The requirements of customers, external and internal, are visibly integrated in the work area.

2-4j   Teams are directly involved in establishing quantitative and qualitative measurements to track the operational effectiveness of the group. This information provides feedback to the teams relating to their overall performance.

2-5 EMPLOYMENT CONTINUITY AND DEVELOPMENT†

Employment continuity is important to the company, as long as the employee exceeds the minimum acceptable job requirements, and the level of business makes it viable.

4—EXCELLENT 3—VERY GOOD 2—FAIR 1—POOR 0—NOT DOING

2-5a   The value of employment continuity is clearly articulated and widely communicated throughout the organization.

☐ ☐ ☐ ☐ ☐

2-5b   Effective employment planning is in place to help reduce the negative effects of rapid change in demand and/or growth and to achieve employment continuity.

☐ ☐ ☐ ☐ ☐

2-5c   There is a clearly defined process for employee selection, induction, and placement, supported by an employee development and a career planning program.

☐ ☐ ☐ ☐ ☐

2-5d   A mechanism exists to re-deploy employees throughout the organization based on their skills and capabilities and the organizational needs.

☐ ☐ ☐ ☐ ☐

2-5e   There is a continuous performance appraisal program based on accomplishments (results-oriented) which simultaneously considers feedback from managers, employees, and other team members.

☐ ☐ ☐ ☐ ☐

4—EXCELLENT 3—VERY GOOD 2—FAIR 1—POOR 0—NOT DOING

☐ ☐ ☐ ☐ ☐

2-6 EDUCATION AND TRAINING†

An active education and training program focused on business issues, customer issues, and operational improvements is in place for all company personnel. Its objectives include enhancing people's skills, increasing process flexibility, sharing tools/ technology understanding, and meeting future needs. Education and training are viewed as a strategic advantage, and the knowledge gained is measured by its successful application to the job.

2-6a   Management views education and training as a strategic advantage, and their attitude and actions demonstrate commitment and involvement to educate and train all necessary people fully prior to implementation of new processes and tools/technologies.

☐ ☐ ☐ ☐ ☐

2-6b   Education and training are aligned with the strategic initiatives to assure the right education and training is done and that it is cost effective.

☐ ☐ ☐ ☐ ☐

2-6c   Education is a participative process flowing in two directions (top to bottom and bottom to top) of the organization.

☐ ☐ ☐ ☐ ☐

4—EXCELLENT 3—VERY GOOD 2—FAIR 1—POOR 0—NOT DOING

2-6d The education and training program recognizes people at all levels as experts in their respective areas. The education program uses these people to communicate company goals and objectives, facilitate the required change process, and measure performance results.

☐ ☐ ☐ ☐ ☐

2-6e The education and training approach is based on the principles of process and behavior change in an organization rather than merely on fact-transfer regarding specific tools or technologies.

☐ ☐ ☐ ☐ ☐

2-6f All education and training sessions clearly define the skills needed for each job, set the expectation that behavior will change, provide a process to assure that those skills are acquired, and hold supervisors/leaders accountable for administering the process.

☐ ☐ ☐ ☐ ☐

2-6g The supervisor/leaders and employee performance evaluations are tied to successful application of the knowledge gained in the education and training sessions.

☐ ☐ ☐ ☐ ☐

2-6h The company has committed adequate resources, time, and finances to education and training.

☐ ☐ ☐ ☐ ☐

4—EXCELLENT 3—VERY GOOD 2—FAIR 1—POOR 0—NOT DOING

2-6i An ongoing education and training program is used to refine and improve the use of business tools such as team-based technologies, integrated business planning processes, software, etc.

☐ ☐ ☐ ☐ ☐

2-6j At least annually, the company education and training schedule is updated and published. This education schedule includes sessions covering company policies/procedures, business processes, hardware/software, skill improvement, safety, health, environment, etc.

☐ ☐ ☐ ☐ ☐

2-6k Areas of people improvement needs are continuously assessed.

☐ ☐ ☐ ☐ ☐

2-6l Company personnel records are updated upon completion of education and training events.

☐ ☐ ☐ ☐ ☐

2-6m A reference library containing published materials, education videos, computer aided instruction disks, reference manuals, video support materials, etc. is in place to assist people in their skill development. Policies and procedures are implemented to ensure availability and maintenance of library materials.

☐ ☐ ☐ ☐ ☐

4—EXCELLENT   3—VERY GOOD   2—FAIR   1—POOR   0—NOT DOING

2-7 WORK DESIGN†
Jobs are designed to reinforce the company goal of a team-based, empowered workforce.

☐ ☐ ☐ ☐ ☐

2-7a   The organizational structure is designed to meet internal and external customer needs and to create flexibility in the decision-making process.

☐ ☐ ☐ ☐ ☐

2-7b   Skill training is formalized and managed to create the desired level of flexibility.

☐ ☐ ☐ ☐ ☐

2-7c   Performance-review sessions are conducted periodically to provide ongoing feedback to teams and individuals.

☐ ☐ ☐ ☐ ☐

2-7d   Behaviors and results that support the business strategy are recognized immediately and rewarded in order to reinforce teams and individual future performance.

☐ ☐ ☐ ☐ ☐

2-8 CONGRUENCE
People policies, organizational development, and education and training are consistent with the company vision, mission, and business strategies.

☐ ☐ ☐ ☐ ☐

2-8a   Everyone in the organization can state the vision, mission, and main business strategy of the company and knows who are the key customers, key competitors, and key suppliers. They can also describe what differentiates the product/service they build/support from others in the marketplace.

☐ ☐ ☐ ☐ ☐

4—EXCELLENT 3—VERY GOOD 2—FAIR 1—POOR 0—NOT DOING

2-8b   The performance-management factors for teams and individuals are reviewed and updated to reflect changes in the business objectives and the work process.   □ □ □ □ □

2-8c   Employee satisfaction and organizational climate measures are taken and monitored periodically. Attributes such as employee attitude, absenteeism, and turnover are measured regularly. Baseline numbers have been established, and positive trends are evident.   □ □ □ □ □

2-8d   The company has the means and the ability to attract, select, motivate, and reward the type of people it needs.   □ □ □ □ □

3
TOTAL QUALITY AND CONTINUOUS IMPROVEMENT PROCESSES

QUALITATIVE CHARACTERISTICS

Class A   There is discontent with the status quo and Total Quality/Continuous Improvement has become a natural way of life for employees, suppliers, and customers. Improved quality in both manufacturing and in support functions, reduced costs, increased velocity, and a focus on the customer has contributed to competitive advantage.

Class B   Most departments, suppliers, and customers are participating in these processes. Substantial improvements have been made in many areas.

Class C   Processes are being utilized in limited areas and with some suppliers. Some improvements have been achieved.

Class D   Processes are either not established or their use is minimal in the ongoing operation of the business.

OVERVIEW ITEMS

3-1 COMMITMENT TO EXCELLENCE

There is a focus on meeting or exceeding both external and internal customer expectations through Total Quality/Continuous Improvement initiatives in reducing lead times, improving the quality of both products and services, and in reducing costs. There is a commitment to the use of Total Quality/Continuous Improvement tools and techniques in all areas of the business. Employee development and employee continuity are stated objectives.

3-2 TOP MANAGEMENT LEADERSHIP FOR QUALITY AND CONTINUOUS IMPROVEMENT

Top executives are actively involved in establishing and communicating the organization's strategy and related goals for the business. The strategy and goals are deployed to ensure that all employees are aware of the organization's vision, plans, goals, and values. Key Performance Indicators [KPI's] for each goal have been established and are reviewed monthly by top management to ensure continuous improvement of all business processes.

3-3 FOCUS ON CUSTOMER

A variety of effective techniques is in active use throughout all areas of the business to ensure that both internal and external customer expectations are identified, prioritized and either met or exceeded.

3-4 CUSTOMER PARTNERSHIPS

Strong "partnership" relationships that are mutually beneficial are being established with key customers.

3-5 CONTINUOUS ELIMINATION OF WASTE

There is demonstrated discontent with the status quo, manifested by a company-wide commitment to the continuous and relentless reduction and elimination of waste. Waste is understood to be any activity that does not add value to the product for the customer. A formal program is used to expose, prioritize, and stimulate the reduction or elimination of these nonvalue-added activities.

3-6 ROUTINE USE OF TOTAL QUALITY/CONTINUOUS IMPROVEMENT TOOLS

Routine use of Total Quality/Continuous Improvement tools has become a way of life in virtually all areas of the company.

3-7 RESOURCES AND FACILITIES—FLEXIBILITY, COST, QUALITY

Resources and facilities required to meet the needs of customers profitablyare continuously being made more flexible, cost effective, and capable of producing higher quality.

3-8 PRODUCE TO CUSTOMER ORDERS

The time required to manufacture products or provide services has been reduced such that the planning and control system is able to use forecasts to project the needs for resources. The production of finished products or provision of services is based on actual customer orders or distribution demands (except where strategic or seasonal inventories are being built).

3-9 SUPPLIER PARTNERSHIPS

Strong "partnership" relationships that are mutually beneficial are being established with fewer but better suppliers.

3-10 PROCUREMENT—QUALITY, RESPONSIVENESS, COST†
The procurement process is continuously being improved and simplified to improve quality and responsiveness while simultaneously reducing the total procurement costs.

3-11 KANBAN
Kanban is being effectively used to control production where its use will provide significant results.

3-12 VELOCITY
The velocity and linearity of workflow is continuously being measured, reported, and improved.

3-13 ACCOUNTING SIMPLIFICATION
Accounting procedures are being simplified, eliminating nonvalue-added activities, while at the same time providing the ability to generate information sufficiently accurate to use in decision making and satisfy audit requirements for the financial control of operations.

3-14 TEAMWORK†
Clearly identifiable teams are utilized as the primary means to direct, organize, and perform the work, as opposed to individual job functions.

3-15 EDUCATION AND TRAINING†
An active education and training program focused on business issues, customer issues, and operational improvements is in place for all company personnel. Its objectives include enhancing people's skills, increasing process flexibility, sharing tools/technology understanding, and meeting future needs. Education and training are viewed as a strategic advantage, and the knowledge gained is measured by its successful application to the job.

3-16 WORK DESIGN†
Jobs are designed to reinforce the company goal of a team-based, em-powered workforce. Work is standardized to ensure consistency of all business processes.

3-17 EMPLOYMENT CONTINUITY†
Employment continuity is of important value to the company as long as the employee exceeds the minimum acceptable job requirements and the level of business makes it viable.

3-18 COMPANY PERFORMANCE—QUALITY, DELIVERY, COST
Company performance measurements emphasize quality, delivery, and cost. Performance measures are communicated to all through visible displays that show progress and point the way to improvement.

3-19 SETTING AND ATTAINING BREAKTHROUGH GOALS
Short- and long-term breakthrough goals that cause the organization to re-engineer or replace current processes are established, regularly re-viewed, and monitored. These breakthrough goals are targeted on im provements in total cost, cycle time (or response time), and customer requirements.

OVERVIEW AND DETAIL ITEMS

3-1 COMMITMENT TO EXCELLENCE*

☐ ☐ ☐ ☐ ☐

There is a focus on meeting or exceeding both external and internal customer expectations through Total Quality/Continuous Improvement initiatives in reducing lead times, improving the quality of both products and services, and in reducing costs. There is a commitment to the use of Total Quality/Continuous Improvement tools and techniques in all areas of the business. Employee development and employee continuity are stated objectives.

3-2 TOP MANAGEMENT LEADERSHIP FOR QUALITY AND CONTINUOUS IMPROVEMENT

☐ ☐ ☐ ☐ ☐

Top executives are actively involved in establishing and communicating the organization's strategy and related goals for the business. The strategy and goals are deployed to ensure that all employees are aware of the organization's vision, plans, goals, and values. Key Performance Indicators [KPI's] for each goal have been established and are reviewed monthly by top management to ensure continuous improvement of all business processes.

3-2a   Top management not only understands Total Quality/Continuous Improvement concepts, but also uses these tools and techniques as part of the management process.

☐ ☐ ☐ ☐ ☐

4—EXCELLENT   3—VERY GOOD   2—FAIR   1—POOR   0—NOT DOING

3-2b   Top management is in routine contact with customers, suppliers, and employees.

☐ ☐ ☐ ☐ ☐

3-2c   Strategies and actions at all levels of management exhibit a belief in Total Quality/ Continuous Improvement.

☐ ☐ ☐ ☐ ☐

3-2d   Resources such as time, money, etc. are provided throughout the organization toward the improvement of quality and innovation.

☐ ☐ ☐ ☐ ☐

3-2e   Employees can articulate their company's strategic goals and focus their improvement activities to support them.

☐ ☐ ☐ ☐ ☐

3-2f   All employees are encouraged to contribute to improvements in processes and systems.

☐ ☐ ☐ ☐ ☐

3-2g   Management monitors the extent to which Total Quality/Continuous Improvement tools and techniques are being utilized and routinely removes barriers to performance, innovation, and quality.

☐ ☐ ☐ ☐ ☐

3-3 FOCUS ON CUSTOMER

☐ ☐ ☐ ☐ ☐

A variety of effective techniques is in active use throughout all areas of the business to ensure that both internal and external customer expectations are identified, prioritized, and either met or exceeded.

4—EXCELLENT 3—VERY GOOD 2—FAIR 1—POOR 0—NOT DOING

3-3a   Strategic market segments are clearly identified and known. There is a clear and written description of the value chain for each segment. The position of the company versus its competitors is formally documented and monitored.

☐ ☐ ☐ ☐ ☐

3-3b   For all internal processes, the process owner, suppliers to the process, and customers of the process have been identified.

☐ ☐ ☐ ☐ ☐

3-3c   Mechanisms for developing both external and internal customer needs and expectations are regularly used.

☐ ☐ ☐ ☐ ☐

3-3d   Management ensures that all employees are aware of customer needs and expectations. Goals have been established, and customer satisfaction is monitored and reported.

☐ ☐ ☐ ☐ ☐

3-3e   There is easy access by customers to information, and problem resolution is assured through customer-contact employees who have sufficient authority and who are empowered to resolve customer issues.

☐ ☐ ☐ ☐ ☐

3-3f   Customer feedback systems are continuously evaluated and improved. Changes in customer patterns are monitored and evaluated as part of this process.

☐ ☐ ☐ ☐ ☐

4—EXCELLENT 3—VERY GOOD 2—FAIR 1—POOR 0—NOT DOING

☐ ☐ ☐ ☐ ☐

3-4 CUSTOMER PARTNERSHIPS

Strong "partnership" relationships that are mutually beneficial are being established with key customers.

3-4a   Marketing and sales view Total Quality/ Continuous Improvement as a competitive weapon in the marketplace.

☐ ☐ ☐ ☐ ☐

3-4b   Long-term, mutually beneficial relationships with customers are being pursued to facilitate improvements in quality, cost, and overall customer satisfaction.

☐ ☐ ☐ ☐ ☐

3-4c   Direct communications between the company's operating departments and the customer's operating departments have been established to simplify processes and to improve responsiveness.

☐ ☐ ☐ ☐ ☐

3-4d   The customer-order fulfillment cycle time is continuously being reduced.

☐ ☐ ☐ ☐ ☐

3-4e   Product replenishment by kanban is being used where applicable.

☐ ☐ ☐ ☐ ☐

3-4f   Total Quality/Continuous Improvement initiatives are encouraged throughout the customer base. Information is freely shared. Goals are agreed upon. Cost savings are shared.

☐ ☐ ☐ ☐ ☐

3-5 CONTINUOUS ELIMINATION OF WASTE

There is demonstrated discontent with the status quo, manifested by a company-wide commitment to the continuous and relentless reduction and elimination of waste. Waste is understood to be any activity that does not add value to the product for the customer. A formal program is used to expose, prioritize, and stimulate the reduction or elimination of these nonvalue-added activities.

3-5a A formal, visible, and continuous process is in place to reduce changeover times, inspection, lead times, lot sizes, redundancy, safety stocks, queues, and all other types of nonvalue-added activities. Employees at all levels and in all areas can articulate the essence of this process and are contributing ideas for, and are participating in, waste-elimination initiatives. Goals have been set. Results are documented and publicized.

3-5b The concept that quality is "built in," not "inspected in," has become a way of life, and separate inspection activities are being reduced or eliminated. Employees are empowered to stop production rather than pass on a known defect.

3-5c A formal and active program exists to reduce scrap, rework, and shrinkage, and to increase yields. Goals have been set. Results are documented and publicized.

3-5d   When appropriate, a Total Productive Maintenance (TPM) process has been implemented. Goals have been set. Results are documented and publicized.

☐ ☐ ☐ ☐ ☐

3-5e   The quantity of item numbers (drawing numbers, part numbers, sku's, etc.) is being reduced through an ongoing standardization initiative.

☐ ☐ ☐ ☐ ☐

3-5f   Engineering changes are analyzed using Total Quality/Continuous Improvement techniques to reduce their number and the associated costs.

☐ ☐ ☐ ☐ ☐

3-5g   Information is available to operations people in a timely manner. A goal exists to simplify, minimize, or eliminate the number of transactions and reports.

☐ ☐ ☐ ☐ ☐

3-6 ROUTINE USE OF TOTAL QUALITY/CONTINUOUS IMPROVEMENT TOOLS

Routine use of Total Quality/Continuous Improvement tools has become a way of life in virtually all areas of the company.

☐ ☐ ☐ ☐ ☐

3-6a   Each functional area has established a set of key internal and/or external customer satisfaction measures, tracks performance, and seeks the root cause of variations.

☐ ☐ ☐ ☐ ☐

3-6b   All members of the organization make decisions based on data.

☐ ☐ ☐ ☐ ☐

4—EXCELLENT
3—VERY GOOD
2—FAIR
1—POOR
0—NOT DOING

3-6c   Cause-and-effect diagrams are used routinely throughout the organization.   ☐ ☐ ☐ ☐ ☐

3-6d   Key problems under attack are shown in visible displays containing information about the team members, root cause and variation analysis, actions, and results.   ☐ ☐ ☐ ☐ ☐

3-6e   Control charts are used where appropriate but are not the only Total Quality/Continuous Improvement tools in evidence.   ☐ ☐ ☐ ☐ ☐

3-6f   Flow charts are used to document key processes in manufacturing and other areas.   ☐ ☐ ☐ ☐ ☐

3-6g   Standardized work practices have been implemented to eliminate process variation. This has become a common practice in all areas of the company.   ☐ ☐ ☐ ☐ ☐

3-6h   Multiple levels of Pareto charts are used to identify the root cause where appropriate.   ☐ ☐ ☐ ☐ ☐

3-6i   Inspection in all areas is viewed as waste. Inspection has been reduced or eliminated as process control has being achieved.   ☐ ☐ ☐ ☐ ☐

3-7 RESOURCES AND FACILITIES— FLEXIBILITY, COST, QUALITY   ☐ ☐ ☐ ☐ ☐
Resources and facilities required to meet the needs of customers profitably are continuously being made more flexible, cost-effective, and capable of producing higher quality.

4—EXCELLENT   3—VERY GOOD   2—FAIR   1—POOR   0—NOT DOING

3-7a   Plant and office layouts are being continuously improved to simplify and reduce the physical transport of material or sharing of information (e.g., distance and handling are minimized; communications and visibility are maximized).   ☐ ☐ ☐ ☐ ☐

3-7b   Equipment is selected based on its contribution to improved quality, fast changeover, minimum lot sizes, flexibility, and overall throughput time. A policy exists to justify equipment based on these factors in addition to traditional selection criteria.   ☐ ☐ ☐ ☐ ☐

3-7c   Authorization for capital spending places high value on the company's drive to improve quality and increase the velocity of product or information from suppliers through the plant and out to the customer.   ☐ ☐ ☐ ☐ ☐

3-7d   Simplified manufacturing processes with visual controls are in place, allowing problems to be identified quickly.   ☐ ☐ ☐ ☐ ☐

3-7e   Tools and fixtures are stored primarily at the point of use, where practical.   ☐ ☐ ☐ ☐ ☐

3-7f   Setup and changeover times are being systematically and continuously reduced, thereby enabling manufacturing lot sizes to be economically reduced.   ☐ ☐ ☐ ☐ ☐

3-7g   Unplanned machine downtime is documented and being reduced.   ☐ ☐ ☐ ☐ ☐

4—EXCELLENT 3—VERY GOOD 2—FAIR 1—POOR 0—NOT DOING

3-7h   Where appropriate, material or information is stored primarily at the point of use and/or at the point of manufacture rather than in a central location.

☐ ☐ ☐ ☐ ☐

3-7i   Good housekeeping (orderliness) is being pursued as a high-priority item by all personnel.

☐ ☐ ☐ ☐ ☐

3-8 PRODUCE TO CUSTOMER ORDERS

☐ ☐ ☐ ☐ ☐

The time required to manufacture products or provide services has been reduced such that the planning and control system is able to use forecasts to project the needs for resources. The production of finished products or provision of services is based on actual customer orders or distribution demands (except where strategic or seasonal inventories are being built).

3-8a   A formal, integrated business process is used to project resource requirements for both plant and suppliers. It is also used to promise customer orders.

☐ ☐ ☐ ☐ ☐

3-8b   Mixed-model scheduling, from master scheduling through the entire manufacturing process and backward into purchasing, is understood and is widely utilized where applicable.

☐ ☐ ☐ ☐ ☐

3-8c   Daily, or shorter, production rates are being emphasized rather than large batches.

☐ ☐ ☐ ☐ ☐

4—EXCELLENT 3—VERY GOOD 2—FAIR 1—POOR 0—NOT DOING

3-8d   The physical movement of materials in the
        factory is triggered by consumption (e.g., a
        kanban signal). One-piece flow, where ap-
        plicable, is an objective.

3-9 SUPPLIER PARTNERSHIPS

Strong "partnership" relationships that are
mutually beneficial are being established with fewer
but better suppliers.

3-9a   The number of suppliers is being continu-
        ously reduced, and single sourcing, where
        practical, is a stated company objective.

3-9b   Supplier selection is based on the total cost
        of acquisition.

3-9c   Long-term (multi-year), mutually benefi-
        cial relationships with suppliers are being
        pursued to facilitate improvements in qual-
        ity, delivery, and cost with key suppliers
        who supply 80% of the purchased volume.

3-9d   Direct communications between the com-
        pany's operating departments and the sup-
        plier's operating departments have been
        established to simplify processes and to
        improve responsiveness.

3-9e   Lead times, from the receipt of the com-
        pany's purchase order at the supplier to re-
        ceipt of the product at the company's
        facility, are continuously being reduced.

4—EXCELLENT 3—VERY GOOD 2—FAIR 1—POOR 0—NOT DOING

3-9f   Material replenishment by kanban autho-   □ □ □ □ □
rization, based on contractual agreement,
is being aggressively pursued with an increasing number of suppliers. A significant
percentage of the purchased volume is already under kanban authorization.

3-9g   Simplified procurement systems are in use   □ □ □ □ □
(supplier schedules, supplier point-of-use
replenishment, purchasing credit cards,
etc.).

3-9h   Key suppliers participate as members of   □ □ □ □ □
the company's new-product development
teams in the development and design
of new products or changes to existing
products.

3-9i   Total Quality/Continuous Improvement   □ □ □ □ □
initiatives are encouraged throughout the
supplier base. Information is freely shared.
Goals are agreed upon. Cost savings are
shared.

3-10 PROCUREMENT—QUALITY, RESPONSIVENESS, COST†   □ □ □ □ □

The procurement process is continuously being improved and simplified to improve quality and responsiveness while simultaneously reducing the total procurement costs.

4—EXCELLENT   3—VERY GOOD   2—FAIR   1—POOR   0—NOT DOING

3-10a   Projections of future requirements for purchased items are shared with suppliers to ensure adequate capacity to support business requirements. These future projections extend beyond the suppliers' quoted lead times.

☐ ☐ ☐ ☐ ☐

3-10b   Suppliers are provided with output reports (e.g., supplier schedules) from the formal planning system.

☐ ☐ ☐ ☐ ☐

3-10c   Purchase-order releases have been reduced or eliminated and replaced by kanban signals for an increasing percentage of the purchased volume.

☐ ☐ ☐ ☐ ☐

3-10d   Suppliers are being certified to reduce/ eliminate source inspection, receiving inspection, and count verification.

☐ ☐ ☐ ☐ ☐

3-10e   Delivery quantities are being economically reduced, resulting in more frequent deliveries of smaller quantities from suppliers.

☐ ☐ ☐ ☐ ☐

3-10f   Transportation costs from suppliers are being decreased even though delivery frequency is being increased.

☐ ☐ ☐ ☐ ☐

3-10g   Where appropriate, materials go directly from dock to point of use rather than from dock to stock. Central stockrooms are viewed primarily as overflow locations.

☐ ☐ ☐ ☐ ☐

4—EXCELLENT   3—VERY GOOD   2—FAIR   1—POOR   0—NOT DOING

3-10h   A supplier rating system has been developed and implemented and is being used to trigger improvements in supplier performance.   ☐ ☐ ☐ ☐ ☐

3-10i   Suppliers practice value analysis/value engineering techniques and make recommendations to improve quality, cost, and responsiveness for both current and new products.   ☐ ☐ ☐ ☐ ☐

3-10j   Direct communications have been established to improve responsiveness between the company's operating departments and the suppliers' operating departments.   ☐ ☐ ☐ ☐ ☐

3-11 KANBAN
Kanban is being effectively used to control production where its use will provide significant results.   ☐ ☐ ☐ ☐ ☐

3-11a   Material is not moved to a workstation that does not have an open kanban.   ☐ ☐ ☐ ☐ ☐

3-11b   Work is not started at a workstation that does not have an open kanban.   ☐ ☐ ☐ ☐ ☐

3-11c   The principal of quality at the sources is understood and has resulted in employees being empowered to stop production rather than pass on a known defect.   ☐ ☐ ☐ ☐ ☐

3-11d   There has been no more than one kanban violation during the last ninety days.   ☐ ☐ ☐ ☐ ☐

3-11e   There have been no more than six ap-   ☐ ☐ ☐ ☐ ☐
proved kanban limit exceptions during the
last twelve months.

3-12 VELOCITY   ☐ ☐ ☐ ☐ ☐
The velocity and linearity of workflow is
continuously being measured, reported, and
improved.

3-12a   A stated company objective is to empha-   ☐ ☐ ☐ ☐ ☐
size improvement in velocity and eliminate
waste in all processes, including but not
limited to, accounting, order entry, design,
procurement, manufacturing, and distribution.

3-12b   Nonmanufacturing processes such as or-   ☐ ☐ ☐ ☐ ☐
der entry, new product development, ac-
counts receivable, and accounts payable
are being simplified to improve velocity in
these areas

3-12c   Process improvements are being made   ☐ ☐ ☐ ☐ ☐
such that routings are being simplified,
and bills of material are being flattened, or
phantom codes are being used to improve
velocity.

3-12d   Production lines are being redesigned to   ☐ ☐ ☐ ☐ ☐
enable mixed-model scheduling with a
minimum of material handling.

4—EXCELLENT
3—VERY GOOD
2—FAIR
1—POOR
0—NOT DOING

3-12e   Functional plant layouts are being replaced with cellular manufacturing where
appropriate.

☐ ☐ ☐ ☐ ☐

3-12f   Lead times in all areas are measured and
reported, and are being reduced.

☐ ☐ ☐ ☐ ☐

3-12g   The time required to close the financial
books each month is measured and reported, and is being reduced.

☐ ☐ ☐ ☐ ☐

3-13 ACCOUNTING SIMPLIFICATION
*Accounting procedures and paperwork are being
simplified, eliminating nonvalue-added activities,
while at the same time providing the ability to
generate information sufficiently accurate to use in
decision making and satisfy audit requirements for
the financial control of operations.*

☐ ☐ ☐ ☐ ☐

3-13a   The use of work orders for the detail track-
ing of labor and material has been either
eliminated or is used only where necessary.

☐ ☐ ☐ ☐ ☐

3-12b   Labor collection procedures are being simplified (e.g., groupings of direct and indi-
rect labor operations, labor collection by
exception, etc.).

☐ ☐ ☐ ☐ ☐

3-13c   Cost drivers in the business are understood
and managed by senior management.

☐ ☐ ☐ ☐ ☐

4—EXCELLENT 3—VERY GOOD 2—FAIR 1—POOR 0—NOT DOING

3-13d   The use of performance measurements has shifted from control to improvement. Those measurements that inhibit versus encourage desired results (labor and machine efficiency, utilization, purchase-price variance, number of rejects by employee, etc.) either have been eliminated or their use has been minimized.

☐ ☐ ☐ ☐ ☐

3-14 TEAMWORK†

☐ ☐ ☐ ☐ ☐

Clearly identifiable teams are utilized as the primary means to direct, organize, and perform the work, as opposed to individual job functions.

3-14a   All team members, managers, supervisors, and technical and support people have been formally introduced to the concepts of high-performance work teams through education.

☐ ☐ ☐ ☐ ☐

3-14b   The roles/jobs have been formally structured to support the work team approach.

☐ ☐ ☐ ☐ ☐

3-14c   Each team has developed a clearly defined charter/mission and operating guidelines.

☐ ☐ ☐ ☐ ☐

3-14d   Each team meets regularly and frequently to solve problems and explore opportunities in its work area.

☐ ☐ ☐ ☐ ☐

4—EXCELLENT 3—VERY GOOD 2—FAIR 1—POOR 0—NOT DOING

3-14e   The work teams and the functions they perform are almost entirely self-contained and managed by the group itself. Group members rely on one another for cross training, problem solving, the handling of administrative duties, and mutual support.

3-14f   A structured method is used by work teams to examine workflow and processes to improve the effectiveness of the operation.

3-14g   Each work group has a defined process for gaining direct feedback from both external and internal customers.

3-14h   The requirements of customers, external and internal, are visible in the work area.

3-14i   Work teams are directly involved in establishing quantitative and qualitative measurements to track the operational effectiveness of the group. This information provides feedback to the teams relating to their overall performance.

3-14j   Quality problems and other opportunities for waste elimination are addressed by a team of the most appropriate people regardless of their reporting level in the organization.

4—EXCELLENT 3—VERY GOOD 2—FAIR 1—POOR 0—NOT DOING

☐ ☐ ☐ ☐ ☐

3-15 EDUCATION AND TRAINING†

An active education and training program focused on business issues, customer issues, and operational improvements is in place for all company personnel. Its objectives include enhancing people's skills, increasing process flexibility, sharing tools/ technology understanding, and meeting future needs. Education and training are viewed as a strategic advantage, and the knowledge gained is measured by its successful application to the job.

3-15a Management views education and training   ☐ ☐ ☐ ☐ ☐
as a strategic advantage, and their attitude and actions demonstrate commitment and involvement to educate and train all necessary people fully prior to implementation of new processes and tools/technologies.

3-15b Education and training are aligned with   ☐ ☐ ☐ ☐ ☐
the strategic initiatives to assure the right education and training is done and that it is cost effective.

3-15c Education is a participative process flow-   ☐ ☐ ☐ ☐ ☐
ing in two directions (top to bottom and bottom to top) of the organization.

3-15d The education and training program rec-   ☐ ☐ ☐ ☐ ☐
ognizes people at all levels as experts in their respective areas. The education program uses these people to communicate company goals and objectives, facilitate the required change processes, and measure performance results.

4—EXCELLENT 3—VERY GOOD 2—FAIR 1—POOR 0—NOT DOING

3-15e   The education and training approach is based on the principles of process and behavior change in an organization rather than merely on fact-transfer regarding specific tools or technologies.

□ □ □ □ □

3-15f   All education and training sessions clearly define the skills needed for each job, set the expectation that behavior will change, provide a process to assure that those skills are acquired and hold supervisors/leaders accountable for administering the process.

□ □ □ □ □

3-15g   The supervisor/leaders and employee performance evaluations are tied to the successful application of the knowledge gained in the education and training sessions.

□ □ □ □ □

3-15h   The company has committed adequate resources, time, and finances to education and training.

□ □ □ □ □

3-15i   An ongoing education and training program is used to refine and improve the use of business tools such as team-based technologies, integrated business planning processes, software, etc.

□ □ □ □ □

3-15j   Periodically, the company education and training schedule is updated and published. This education schedule includes sessions covering company policies/procedures, business processes, hardware/software, skill improvement, safety, health, environment, etc.

□ □ □ □ □

4—EXCELLENT
3—VERY GOOD
2—FAIR
1—POOR
0—NOT DOING

3-15k   Areas of people improvement needs are ☐ ☐ ☐ ☐ ☐
continuously assessed.

3-15l   Company personnel records are updated ☐ ☐ ☐ ☐ ☐
upon completion of education and train-
ing events.

3-15m   A reference library containing published ☐ ☐ ☐ ☐ ☐
materials, education videos, computer
aided instruction disks, reference manuals,
video support materials, etc., is in place to
assist people in their skill development.
Policies and procedures are implemented
to ensure availability and maintenance of
library materials.

3-16 WORK DESIGN†   ☐ ☐ ☐ ☐ ☐

Jobs are designed to reinforce the company goal
of a team-based, empowered workforce. Work is
standardized to ensure consistency of all business
processes.

3-16a   Skill training is formalized and managed ☐ ☐ ☐ ☐ ☐
to create the desired level of flexibility.

3-16b   A performance management system is in ☐ ☐ ☐ ☐ ☐
place to provide ongoing feedback to
teams and individuals.

3-16c   A compensation strategy exists that rec- ☐ ☐ ☐ ☐ ☐
ognizes, rewards, and reinforces behav-
iors and results that support the business
strategy.

3-17 EMPLOYMENT CONTINUITY†

□ □ □ □ □

Employment continuity is of important value to the company as long as the employee exceeds the minimum acceptable job requirements and the level of business makes it viable.

3-17a   The goal of employment continuity is clearly articulated and widely communicated throughout the organization.

□ □ □ □ □

3-17b   Effective employment planning is in place to help reduce the negative effects of rapid change in demand and/or growth and achieve the goal of employment continuity.

□ □ □ □ □

3-18 COMPANY PERFORMANCE— QUALITY, DELIVERY, COST

□ □ □ □ □

Company performance measurements emphasize quality, delivery, and cost. Performance measures are communicated to all through visible displays that show progress and point the way to improvement.

3-18a   Valid, timely information is collected and analyzed on all products and services for external customers and significant and targeted internal customers and suppliers.

□ □ □ □ □

3-18b   A data-and-information collection process exists measuring all aspects of the organization's processes, customers, and suppliers. The data is focused and comprehensive. Any data and information collected has a specific purpose known by the data collectors and generators.

□ □ □ □ □

3-18c Information collected is timely, useful, accurate, and complete. Benchmark data exists for comparative purposes.

□ □ □ □ □

3-18d Routine, periodic checks are made to ensure the validity of data and information collected.

□ □ □ □ □

3-18e Appropriate, advanced technologies and tools are used in all data-and-information collection processes.

□ □ □ □ □

3-18f Objectives have been established for production defects. Performance is measured, and goals are being achieved.

□ □ □ □ □

3-18g Quality measure includes parts per million (PPM) defect reporting where appropriate and cost-of-quality reporting.

□ □ □ □ □

3-18h Objectives have been established for production and supplier defects. Performance is measured, and goals are being achieved.

□ □ □ □ □

3-18i Objectives have been set for cost of quality. Performance is measured, and goals are being achieved.

□ □ □ □ □

3-18j Delivery measures include linearity of output and on-time deliveries.

□ □ □ □ □

4—EXCELLENT 3—VERY GOOD 2—FAIR 1—POOR 0—NOT DOING

3-18k The following measures have been eliminated or deemphasized:

- Labor efficiency (or derivations)
- Machine utilization (or derivations)
- Defects per person
- Purchased part price variance
- Manufacturing overhead rate

3-18l Operating results are posted in a timely manner and made visible to company employees.

3-18m Key measures are usually shown with additional information that points the way to improvements (e.g., run charts plus multilevel Pareto charts).

3-18n Cost measures include inventory days on hand (or turns) and total asset turnover.

3-18o Manufacturing cost-of-quality reports are presented as a routine part of management reporting. While it is difficult to obtain all costs of quality, at least the tangible numbers for appraisal, failure, and prevention are reported.

3-18p The concept of cost of quality is understood in nonmanufacturing areas and reported when practical.

☐ ☐ ☐ ☐ ☐

3-19 SETTING AND ATTAINING BREAKTHROUGH GOALS

Short- and long-term breakthrough goals that cause the organization to re-engineer or replace current processes are established, regularly reviewed, and monitored. These breakthrough goals are targeted on improvements in total cost, cycle time (or response time), and customer requirements.

3-19a Operational plans for achieving improved quality, improved response time, and reduced total cost goals carry clear priorities and accountability.

☐ ☐ ☐ ☐ ☐

3-19b A formal process for establishing these goals and plans exists and is followed.

☐ ☐ ☐ ☐ ☐

3-19c Both intuitive and quantitative information are used to identify areas of improvement. Benchmarking, customer requirements, process capability, and supplier requirements are regularly employed in this process.

☐ ☐ ☐ ☐ ☐

3-19d Customers' expressed, expected, and exciting needs, gaps, and issues are integrated into the planning process for both products and processes.

☐ ☐ ☐ ☐ ☐

3-19e Benchmark data establishing best-in-class practices are used to establish improvement planning for quality initiatives.

☐ ☐ ☐ ☐ ☐

3-19f All levels of the organization participate in the improvement planning process.

☐ ☐ ☐ ☐ ☐

4—EXCELLENT
3—VERY GOOD
2—FAIR
1—POOR
0—NOT DOING

3-19g   Key requirements in technology, training
and education, and supplier quality are
regularly assessed and factored into the
plans. Future targets and current status are
part of the factoring and prioritizing process.

☐ ☐ ☐ ☐ ☐

3-19h   An evaluation of the integrated business-
planning processes is periodically conducted and targeted for improvement and
corrective action.

☐ ☐ ☐ ☐ ☐

4
NEW PRODUCT DEVELOPMENT PROCESSES

QUALITATIVE CHARACTERISTICS

Class A   All functions in the organization are involved with and actively support the product development process. Product requirements are derived from customer needs. Products are developed in significantly shorter time periods, meet these requirements, and require little or no support. Internal and external suppliers are involved in and are an active part of the development process. The resulting revenue and margins satisfy the projections of the original business plan proposals.

Class B   Design engineering (or R&D) and other functions are involved in the development process. Product requirements are derived from customer needs. Product development times have been reduced. A low to medium level of support is required. Few design changes are required for products to meet the requirements.

Class C   The product development process is primarily an engineering or R&D activity. Products are introduced close to schedule but contain traditional problems in manufacturing and the marketplace. Products require significant support to meet performance, quality, or operating objectives. The manufacturing process is not optimized for internal or external suppliers. Some improvement in reducing development time has been achieved.

Class D   The products developed consistently do not meet schedule dates or performance, cost, quality, or reliability goals. They require high levels of support. There is little or no internal or external supplier involvement.

OVERVIEW ITEMS

4-1 COMMITMENT TO EXCELLENCE

There is an intense commitment to excel in the innovation, effectiveness, and speed of new product development. This commitment is broadly shared throughout the organization and is reflected in the company product development strategy. There is a defined, consistent product development process to execute the strategy. Product development quickly produces designs for products/services that meet customer, timeframe, and profit requirements. The intense commitment to excel in new product development is demonstrated by outstanding cycle time, operating margins, design quality, development productivity, and customer advantage performance.

4-2 PRODUCT DEVELOPMENT STRATEGY

The product development strategy defines and advances development goals that improve business viability and competitive standing. The product development strategy is designed to make product development a sustainable competitive advantage.

4-3 AGGREGATE PROJECT PLANNING

Planning and control disciplines are employed to ensure that aggregate development scheduling and resource allocation are consistent with the product development strategy. The aggregate development project planning process is used to support company sales and operations planning.

4-4 CUSTOMER REQUIREMENTS

Customer requirements are the fundamental drivers of product development. Formal methods, such as Quality Function Deployment (QFD) and involving customers or customer representatives in prototyping, are employed to ensure definition of useful requirements. Formal techniques, such as competitive benchmarking, are used to compare product functionality with competitors. Customer requirements include consideration of the product delivery system.

4-5 ACCELERATED PRODUCT DEVELOPMENT

Accelerated product development is achieved through parallel execution of product and process design. This parallel execution is achieved through the use of cross-functional teams working to define customer requirements and product specifications and operating within a well defined planning and control discipline.

4-6 DESIGN QUALITY, MANUFACTURABILITY

Design quality defines products that consistently and reliably meet customer needs under all intended operating conditions throughout the product's intended life. Design quality includes fundamental procedures and methods to ensure quality at the source of the design work; a structured prototyping process to demonstrate systematic progress toward achieving customer requirements; formal disciplines to minimize product functional variation; and formal methods to ensure manufacturable designs.

4-7 DESIGN-TO-ORDER

There is a clear distinction between basic product design and features that can be designed to individual customer orders. Design-to-order is recognized as a different process from base-product design. The design-to-order process quickly produces designs that meet customer and profit requirements. Projects start and operate with clear project objectives, defined tasks, schedules, and resources. Project planning and control is appropriately integrated with manufacturing planning and control. The combination of the design and project management disciplines results in high design productivity and excellent performance to customer commitments.

4-8 DATA MANAGEMENT

It is recognized that information and data are the output from product development activities. The information and data are used by manufacturing, service, quality, sales, customer, supplier, and finance functions. There are data management procedures and activities to ensure proper design, data creation, control, and communication and that the needs of the using functions are met.

4-9 CUSTOMER AND SUPPLIER CONNECTIVITY

Customers, company, and suppliers are considered as one continuum of solutions designed to make our customers' customers successful. There is a company commitment to execute this continuum through customer and supplier focus throughout the organization and involving both customers and suppliers in product planning and development.

4-10 EDUCATION AND TRAINING†

An active education and training program focused on business issues, customer issues, and operational improvements is in place for all company personnel. Its objectives include enhancing people's skills, increasing process flexibility, sharing tools/technology understanding, and meeting future needs. Education and training are viewed as a strategic advantage, and the knowledge gained is measured by its successful application to the job.

4-11 DEVELOPMENT RESULTS

The intense commitment to excel in the innovation, effectiveness, and speed of new product development is demonstrated by outstanding performance in the following areas:

- Cycle times
- Operating margin
- Design quality and development productivity
- Customer advantage

Measurements are used to diagnose problems, assess performance versus goals and competition, and to stimulate continuous process improvements. Performance measures, including this checklist, are not used to rate personnel.

OVERVIEW AND DETAIL ITEMS

4-1 COMMITMENT TO EXCELLENCE*

There is an intense commitment to excel in the innovation, effectiveness, and speed of new product development. This commitment is broadly shared throughout the organization and is reflected in the company product development strategy. There is a defined, consistent product development process to execute the strategy. Product development quickly produces designs for products/services that meet customer, timeframe, and profit requirements. The intense commitment to excel in new product development is demonstrated by outstanding cycle time, operating margins, design quality, development productivity, and customer advantage performance.

4—EXCELLENT
3—VERY GOOD
2—FAIR
1—POOR
0—NOT DOING

4-2 PRODUCT DEVELOPMENT STRATEGY

☐ ☐ ☐ ☐ ☐

The product development strategy defines and advances development goals that improve business viability and competitive standing. The product development strategy is designed to make product development a sustainable competitive advantage.

4-2a   The product development strategy is an integral part of the company business and competitive strategies. Strategy formulation involves senior management plus product development, marketing, manufacturing, and financial management and includes all elements of the organization. Where appropriate, key customers are directly involved in strategy formulation.

☐ ☐ ☐ ☐ ☐

4-2b   There is a product/marketing strategy which clearly links present and planned products to target customers and markets. The product/marketing strategy is supported by company core competencies and technology, and is the basis for the company's product-presence in the marketplace.

☐ ☐ ☐ ☐ ☐

4-2c   There is a clear definition of the core technologies and competencies needed to realize the product development strategy. This definition is based on a realistic understanding of present competencies and a similarly realistic plan for acquiring new competencies.

☐ ☐ ☐ ☐ ☐

4—EXCELLENT
3—VERY GOOD
2—FAIR
1—POOR
0—NOT DOING

4-2d   The product development strategy provides a clear sense of direction to the business, the market, critical development
functions, and all active and proposed development projects. Communicating the
development strategy provides a pervasive
sense of futurity in development decisions.

4-3 AGGREGATE PROJECT PLANNING

*Planning and control disciplines are employed to
ensure that aggregate development scheduling and
resource allocation are consistent with the product
development strategy. The aggregate development
project planning process is integrated with company
sales and operations planning.*

4-3a   Planned project results, schedules, and resource requirements are periodically reviewed for consistency with the product
development strategy.

4-3b   New product-development-project completion requirements are linked to customer commitments and manufacturing,
and to supply-chain capabilities monthly in
the sales and operations planning process.

4—EXCELLENT 3—VERY GOOD 2—FAIR 1—POOR 0—NOT DOING

☐ ☐ ☐ ☐ ☐

4-4 CUSTOMER REQUIREMENTS

Customer requirements are the fundamental drivers of product development. Formal methods, such as Quality Function Deployment (QFD) and involving customers or customer representatives in prototyping, are employed to ensure definition of useful requirements. Formal techniques, such as competitive benchmarking, are used to compare product functionality with competitors. Customer requirements include consideration of the product delivery system.

4-4a Customer requirements are determined utilizing formal voice-of-customer processes, such as in-context interviews, choice modeling, consumer's panels, and competitive benchmarking.

☐ ☐ ☐ ☐ ☐

4-4b Customer requirements are determined for all steps of actual or future value chain. Determination of supply and distribution methods is part of the new product process.

☐ ☐ ☐ ☐ ☐

4-4c Product specifications are produced through formal processes such as Quality Function Deployment (QFD) to link documented customer requirements with customer attributes and design parameters.

☐ ☐ ☐ ☐ ☐

4-4d   The customer requirements process results in clear product vision and objectives focused on customer needs for all development projects. Product differentiation in the marketplace and in the eyes of the customer is clearly delineated at the onset of each development project.

□ □ □ □ □

4-5 ACCELERATED PRODUCT DEVELOPMENT

□ □ □ □ □

Accelerated product development is achieved through parallel execution of product and process design. This parallel execution is achieved through the use of cross-functional teams working to define customer requirements and product specifications and operating within a well defined planning and control discipline.

4-5a   Cross-functional, concurrent product development teams are used to produce error-free product and process designs that meet customer requirements and facilitate quick and complete product introduction.

□ □ □ □ □

4-5b   Cross-functional teams operate across all phases of product development, including such early phases as proposal, concept development, architecture, etc. This early involvement is recognized as essential to creating compatible product requirements and process capabilities; high-quality, manufacturable designs; and reduced development and build times.

□ □ □ □ □

4—EXCELLENT
3—VERY GOOD
2—FAIR
1—POOR
0—NOT DOING

4-5c   Cross-functional product development teams operate within a well-defined planning and control discipline. Development project management is based on definition of deliverables, tasks, schedules, and resources. Project management includes the ability to manage the aggregate resource requirements needed to produce all the development deliverables to schedule. Development planning and control is integrated with supply planning and control.

□ □ □ □ □

4-5d   The product development unit of performance is the cross-functional development team. Accountabilities, rewards, skill development, and company management support cross-functional teams. Teams are held accountable for meeting development project objectives.

□ □ □ □ □

4-6 DESIGN QUALITY, MANUFACTURABILITY

□ □ □ □ □

Design quality defines products that consistently and reliably meet customer needs under all intended operating conditions throughout the product's intended life. Design quality include fundamental procedures and methods to ensure quality at the source of the design work; a structured prototyping process to demonstrate systematic progress toward achieving customer requirements; formal disciplines for minimizing product functional variation; and formal methods to ensure manufacturable designs.

4—EXCELLENT
3— VERY GOOD
2— FAIR
1— POOR
0—NOT DOING

4-6a   There are well-defined procedures and □ □ □ □ □
standards to ensure design quality at the
source of the design work. Development
teams use these procedures to demonstrate
design correctness and completeness.

4-6b   Designs incorporate preferred compo- □ □ □ □ □
nents, processes, and materials. Preferred
components are defined according to company and industry standards and represent
customer, design-engineering, quality,
manufacturing, and field-service requirements. Preferred components, processes,
and materials are supported by a suitable
database and control procedures.

4-6c   Cycles of design, prototype, and test se- □ □ □ □ □
quences are used to incrementally study
product functionality, customer needs,
and manufacturability options. Prototyping cycles are planned and designed to produce the product-and-process learning
needed to develop high-quality products.

4-6d   Systematic methods such as quality func- □ □ □ □ □
tion deployment, robust design, design of
experiments, and process capabilities stud-
ies are used to minimize functional and
process variation.

4-6e   Design for Manufacturability is based on defined, planned, or existing manufacturing processes; identified connections between design choices and manufacturing performance; and establishing the impact between key attributes of product architecture and overall manufacturing performance. The following factors are evaluated as part of Design for Manufacturability:

- Labor and material costs minimized.
- Quality of component parts, fabrication, assembly, testing, and service improved.
- Use of preferred components, processes, and materials. These preferred components, processes, and materials represent the requirements of customers, design engineering, quality, manufacturing, suppliers, and field service.
- Support by integrated data sets and tools for product design, process design, and analysis of customer requirements.
- First-pass manufacturing yields and early field performance are measured and are continuously and significantly improving for new products.

4—EXCELLENT 3—VERY GOOD 2—FAIR 1—POOR 0—NOT DOING
☐ ☐ ☐ ☐ ☐

4-7 DESIGN-TO-ORDER

There is a clear distinction between basic product design and features that can be designed to individual customer orders. Design-to-order is recognized as a different process from base-product design. The design-to-order process quickly produces designs that meet customer and profit requirements. Projects start and operate with clear project objectives, defined tasks, schedules, and resources. Project planning and control is appropriately integrated with manufacturing planning and control. The combination of the design and project management disciplines results in high design productivity and excellent performance to customer commitments.

4-7a   There is clear definition of what portion of the product is base design and what components of the product can be adapted to customer orders. This definition is agreed upon by and understood by marketing, sales, engineering, manufacturing, and senior management and is communicated to the marketplace.

☐ ☐ ☐ ☐ ☐

4-7b   Design disciplines, standards, and project management practices are developed and deployed to continuously increase customer benefits and reduce the time from order placement to order shipment.

☐ ☐ ☐ ☐ ☐

4-7c   The design-to-order process balances customer requirements with manufacturing and supplier capabilities to produce projects that deliver what customers ordered on the date requested.

4-7d   Project planning and control disciplines are deployed to ensure that design-to-order project schedules and resource allocation are consistent with both customer commitments and the company business strategies.

4-7e   Project management is based on design-to-order teams operating with well-defined project objectives, deliverables, tasks, schedules, and resources. Project-team management is consistent with team roles and accountabilities. An active lessons-learned function uses project performance to improve the design-to-order process. Project management includes the ability to manage the aggregate resource requirements needed to produce all the designs to schedule.

4-7f   Due dates for design deliverables are derived from master schedule commitments. Design activities' due dates are linked to corresponding manufacturing need dates. Design-to-order capacity planning is deployed to ensure that design schedules are achievable.

4-7g   Aggregate, design-to-order requirements and capacity are analyzed as part of the sales-and-operations planning process.

$\square$ $\square$ $\square$ $\square$ $\square$

4-8 DATA MANAGEMENT

$\square$ $\square$ $\square$ $\square$ $\square$

It is recognized that information and data are the output from product development activities. The information and data are used by manufacturing, service, quality, sales, customer, supplier, and finance functions. There are data management procedures and activities to ensure proper design, data creation, control, and communication and that the needs of the using functions are met.

4-8a   Product development teams are supported by product- and process-definition databases. There is a comprehensive set of design document standards and a controlled method for distributing design information.

$\square$ $\square$ $\square$ $\square$ $\square$

4-8b   There is an effective process for evaluating, planning, documenting, and controlling changes to the existing products.

$\square$ $\square$ $\square$ $\square$ $\square$

4-8c   The company recognizes that the past can assist future product development. Technical, procedural, resource, and scheduling data are captured and utilized as a key learnings database to form a lessons-learned database to improve future designs and the product development process.

$\square$ $\square$ $\square$ $\square$ $\square$

4-9 CUSTOMER AND SUPPLIER CONNECTIVITY

*Customers, company, and suppliers are considered
as one continuum of solutions designed to make
our customers' customers successful. There is a
company commitment to execute this continuum
through customer and supplier focus throughout the
organization and involving both customers and
suppliers in product planning and development.*

4-9a   The goal of the company product development process is to produce products that
make our customers' customers successful. The process to determine customer
needs is continuously improved. A variety
of effective techniques is used to ensure
that customer needs are identified, prioritized, and satisfied. Central to the cus-
tomer-need definition process is the ability
to understand and solve the problems our
customers face in their efforts to make
their customers successful.

4-9b   The supplier base is recognized as a prime
source of technology and quality products.
Supplier partners are involved in new
product and new technology planning and
development. Product designs and associated product definitions are continually
evaluated for their ability to meet supplier
needs.

☐ ☐ ☐ ☐ ☐

4-10 EDUCATION AND TRAINING

An active education and training program focused on business issues, customer issues, and operational improvements is in place for all company personnel. Its objectives include enhancing people's skills, increasing process flexibility, sharing tools/ technology understanding, and meeting future needs. Education and training are viewed as a strategic advantage, and the knowledge gained is measured by its successful application to the job.

4-10a Management views education and training   ☐ ☐ ☐ ☐ ☐
as a strategic advantage, and their attitude and actions demonstrate commitment and involvement to educate and train all necessary people fully prior to implementation of new processes and tools/technologies.

4-10b Education and training are aligned with   ☐ ☐ ☐ ☐ ☐
the strategic initiatives to assure the right education and training is done and that it is cost effective.

4-10c Education is a participative process flow-   ☐ ☐ ☐ ☐ ☐
ing in two directions (top to bottom and bottom to top) of the organization.

4-10d The education and training program rec-   ☐ ☐ ☐ ☐ ☐
ognizes people at all levels as experts in their respective areas. The education program uses these people to communicate company goals and objectives, facilitate the required change process, and measure performance results.

4—EXCELLENT 3—VERY GOOD 2—FAIR 1—POOR 0—NOT DOING

4-10e   The education and training approach is based on the principles of process and behavior change in an organization rather than merely on fact-transfer regarding specific tools or technologies.

☐ ☐ ☐ ☐ ☐

4-10f   All education and training sessions clearly define the skills needed for each job, set the expectation that behavior will change, provide a process to assure that those skills are acquired, and hold supervisors/leaders accountable for administering the process.

☐ ☐ ☐ ☐ ☐

4-10g   The supervisor/leaders and employee performance evaluations are tied to successful application of the knowledge gained in the education and training sessions on the job.

☐ ☐ ☐ ☐ ☐

4-10h   The company has committed adequate resources, time, and finances to education and training.

☐ ☐ ☐ ☐ ☐

4-10i   An ongoing education and training program is used to refine and improve the use of business tools such as team-based technologies, integrated business planning processes, software, etc.

☐ ☐ ☐ ☐ ☐

4-10j   Periodically, the company education and training schedule is updated and published. This education schedule includes sessions covering company policies/procedures, business processes, hardware/software, skill improvement, safety, health, environment, etc.

☐ ☐ ☐ ☐ ☐

4—EXCELLENT
3—VERY GOOD
2—FAIR
1—POOR
0—NOT DOING

4-10k Areas of people improvement needs are continuously assessed. ☐ ☐ ☐ ☐ ☐

4-10l Company personnel records are updated upon completion of education and training events. ☐ ☐ ☐ ☐ ☐

4-10m A reference library containing published materials, education videos, computer aided instruction disks, reference manuals, video support materials, etc., is in place to assist people in their skill development. Policies and procedures are implemented to ensure availability and maintenance of library materials. ☐ ☐ ☐ ☐ ☐

4-11 DEVELOPMENT RESULTS ☐ ☐ ☐ ☐ ☐
The intense commitment to excel in the innovation, effectiveness, and speed of new product development is demonstrated by outstanding performance in the following areas:

- *Cycle times*
- *Operating margins*
- *Design quality and development productivity*
- *Customer advantage*

Measurements are used to diagnose problems, assess performance versus goals and competition, and to stimulate continuous process improvements. Performance measures, including this checklist, are not used to rate personnel.

Cycle Times

4-11a   Time is viewed as a competitive weapon and as a fundamental driver of product development improvements. A major part of development effectiveness is the continual reduction in the time-to-market and product-build times.

4-11b   *Time-to-market.* The time from product concept to product break-even is measured and is continuously reduced. The following components are measured and improving.

- the time from product concept to introduction.
- the time from product introduction to break-even.
- the time from concept to break-even.

4-11c   *The product lead time.* The time taken to buy components and to build, test, and ship products is being continually reduced through product and process design improvements.

4-11d   *Performance-to-development schedule.* A performance-to-development schedule of at least 95% on-time completions is recognized as a foundation for cycle-time improvement and is occurring.

4-11e   *Percent yearly revenues from new products.* The ability to introduce multiple products quickly is being measured by the percent of yearly revenues attributable to new products.

Operating Margins

4-11f   Operating margins (the difference between
price and cost) are recognized as a critical
measure of company viability. Product designs consistently meet profit projections.
The ability to gain premium pricing is continually pursued and product and product-
line costs are continuously reduced.

4-11g   *Product and product-line profitability.* The
profitability of products and product line is
continually measured and improved versus
goals and competition. The following elements are measured and improving:

- product and product-line profitability.
- lack of or reduction in product and
  product-line discounting.
- dollar value of price premiums by product and product line.

4-11h   *Ability to meet margin goals.* Comparison
of margin estimates made at the beginning
of design are compared to margins actu-
ally achieved. This comparison is used to
improve both the estimating process and
the development process.

4-11i   *Product and life-cycle cost reduction.* Both
product and life-cycle cost objectives are
established for products and product lines.
Progress toward these objectives is continuously measured and improved during the
development process and following product release.

Design Quality and Development Productivity

4-11j   Customer and factory performance data
are used to verify that company products
reliably deliver intended performance over
the full range of intended operating environments. Design quality is measured and
improving throughout the design, build,
and service cycle. Product development
satisfies internal customers by providing
error-free design information in a timely
fashion. The company leverages development skills and core competencies. This
leverage is demonstrated by an increasing
number and breadth of successful projects
completed per time period per work group.

☐ ☐ ☐ ☐ ☐

4-11k   *Design quality.* Measures of quality at the
source of design work and the effectiveness
of the prototyping cycle are used to improve the quality of basic design work. The
effectiveness of prototyping to detect
problems early in the design cycle is measured. Factory and field quality problems
are diagnosed, and the results are used to
improve designs. The following elements
are measured and are improving:

☐ ☐ ☐ ☐ ☐

• Errors detected in design proofing and
validation are diagnosed for cause, and
the results are used to improve design
processes.
• Measures are devised and used to determine and improve the effectiveness of
both individual prototyping cycles and

the overall prototype cycle. The measures are designed to improve the amount and scope of learning and to detect requirements and design problems early in the development cycle.

• Factory and field failures are diagnosed for design problems. Causal analysis is performed to correct or improve design quality and the development process.

• Costs of non-quality are measured in development, in the factory, at suppliers, and in the field. The cost analysis is used to drive improvements in failure prevention.

4-111 *Development productivity.* The company return on development skills and core competencies is demonstrated by the number and breadth of successful projects completed per time period. The following elements are measured and improving:

• the number of products completed on time and within budget.
• performance-to-budget.
• the number and scope of products produced from identified core competencies.
• the number of product introductions per development team and development team member per time period.

4-11m   *Design information effectiveness.* The accuracy and timeliness of design information is continuously evaluated and improved by development, manufacturing, field service, and sales functions. The results are used to improve the quality of design information. The following are measured and improving:

- The number, scope, and duration of design changes is being reduced.
- The accuracy of design documents, such as bills of material, drawings, and specifications, is being improved.

Customer Advantage

4-11n   There is visible market evidence that the company creates products that "help our customers make their customers successful," This evidence includes meeting product/market share and revenue objectives, and measured and validated contributions to our customers' value add.

4-11o   There is tangible evidence that company products are achieving an improving market approval. The following elements are measured and are improving:

- market share by product and product line.
- product/market share and revenue performance versus product/market objectives.
- competitive comparison of product and product-line functionality, distinctiveness, and performance.

4-11p   *Make our customers' customers more successful.* There are quantified measures for the contribution of company products to our customers' value add. These measures are used to drive the product development strategy and improve the product development process. The following are measured and improving:

- Customer satisfaction.
- Customer retention. This measure includes customer duration, the number of repeat sales, and customer penetration versus our product-line offering.
- Contribution to customer value add. For key customers, achievement of their customer satisfaction goals and product/ market objectives is related to our product contribution to the customer value add.

5

PLANNING AND CONTROL PROCESSES

QUALITATIVE CHARACTERISTICS

Class A Planning and control processes are effectively used company wide, from top to bottom. Their use generates significant improvements in customer, employee, and stakeholder satisfaction as well as in customer service, productivity, inventory, and costs.

Class B These processes are supported by top management and used by middle management to achieve measurable company improvements; opportunities still exist to upgrade planning and control as a whole.

Class C The planning and control system is operated primarily as a better method for ordering materials; its contribution is to improve production and inventory management.

Class D Information provided by the planning and control system is inaccurate and poorly understood by users; it provides little help in running the business.

OVERVIEW ITEMS

5-1 COMMITMENT TO EXCELLENCE
There is a commitment by top management and throughout the company to use effective planning and control processes and tools. A single set of numbers is used by all members of the organization. These numbers represent valid plans that people believe and use to run the business.

5-2 SALES AND OPERATIONS PLANNING
There is a Sales and Operations Planning (S&OP) process in place that maintains a valid, current operating plan in support of customer requirements and the business plan. This process includes a formal meeting each month run by the general manager and covers a planning horizon adequate to plan resources effectively.

5-3 FINANCIAL PLANNING, REPORTING, AND MEASUREMENT
There is a single set of numbers used by all functions within the operating environment which provides the source data used for financial planning, reporting, and measurement.

5-4 ACCOUNTABLE FORECASTING PROCESS
There is a process for forecasting all anticipated demands with sufficient detail and an adequate planning horizon to support business planning, sales and operations planning, and master scheduling. Forecast accuracy is measured and appropriate action taken in order to continuously improve the accuracy and forecast process.

5-5 SALES PLANS
There is a formal sales planning process in place with sales and marketing responsible and accountable for developing and executing the resulting sales/bookings plan. Differences between the sales plan and actual sales are reconciled, and sales plan performance is measured.

5-6 CUSTOMER PLANNING AND SATISFACTION

Customer order entry and promising are integrated with master scheduling and inventory management. There are mechanisms for matching incoming orders to forecasts, handling abnormal demands, and making sound delivery commitments based on a valid master schedule as well as accurate inventory data.

5-7 MASTER SCHEDULING

The master scheduling process is perpetually managed in order to ensure a balance of stability and responsiveness. The master schedule is reconciled monthly with the production plan resulting from the sales and operations planning process.

5-8 MATERIAL PLANNING AND CONTROL

There is a material planning process that maintains valid material schedules along with a control process that communicates priorities through production schedules, supplier schedules, and/or kanban mechanisms.

5-9 SUPPLIER PLANNING AND CONTROL

A supplier planning and scheduling process provides visibility for key items over an adequate planning horizon. A supply management process exists that ensures effective control of the established supply chain.

5-10 CAPACITY PLANNING AND CONTROL

There is a capacity planning process using rough-cut capacity planning and, where applicable, capacity requirements planning in which planned capacity, based on demonstrated output, is balanced with required capacity. A capacity control process is used to measure and manage manufacturing requirements, work throughput, and queue levels.

5-11 PRODUCTION PLANNING AND CONTROL

There is a planning process supported by a control process that creates, maintains, and synchronizes detailed production schedules. These synchronized schedules communicate valid manufacturing priorities via electronic computer screens, dispatch lists, schedule boards, and/or kanban mechanisms.

5-12 CUSTOMER SERVICE

An objective for on-time deliveries exists and customers are in agreement with it. Performance against the objective is measured and results confirm that performance to defined fill rates and/or promised delivery dates is 95–100%. Graphs or charts showing actual performance versus plan are maintained along with the appropriate analysis, highlighting the primary causes of all deviations outside established and management approved tolerances.

5-13 SALES PLAN PERFORMANCE

Accountability is established by measuring sales performance to plan. Sales plans are directly aligned to support the S&OP process. Performance metrics for sales plan performance are in alignment with other operating metrics. Graphs or charts showing actual performance versus plan are maintained along with the appropriate analysis, highlighting the primary causes of all deviations outside established and management approved tolerances.

5-14 PRODUCTION PLAN PERFORMANCE

Accountability for production plan performance has been established, and the goals and method of measurement agreed upon. All goals, metrics, and performance results are communicated to appropriate company functions. Production plan performance is within ± 2% of the monthly plan by product family, except in produce-to-order environments when demand is less than plan. In this case, the performance is within ± 2% of the demand. If a change in the production plan is authorized by top management, the measure is made against the newly authorized plan. Graphs or charts showing actual performance versus plan are maintained along with the appropriate analysis, highlighting the primary causes of all deviations outside established and management approved tolerances.

5-15 MASTER SCHEDULE PERFORMANCE

Accountability for master schedule performance has been established, and the goals and method of measurement agreed upon. All goals, metrics, and performance results are communicated to appropriate company functions. Master schedule performance is 95–100% of the plan. Graphs or charts showing actual performance versus plan are maintained along with the appropriate analysis, highlighting the primary causes of all deviations outside established and management approved tolerances.

5-16 MANUFACTURING SCHEDULE PERFORMANCE

Accountability for manufacturing schedule performance has been established, and the goals and method of measurement agreed upon. All goals, metrics, and performance results are communicated to appropriate company functions. Manufacturing schedule performance is 95–100% of the plan. Graphs or charts showing actual performance versus plan are maintained along with the appropriate analysis, highlighting the primary causes of all deviations outside established and management approved tolerances.

5-17 SUPPLIER DELIVERY PERFORMANCE

Accountability for supplier delivery performance has been established, and the goals and method of measurement have been agreed upon. All goals, metrics, and performance results are communicated to appropriate company functions. Supplier delivery performance is 95–100% of the plan. Graphs or charts showing actual performance versus plan are maintained along with the appropriate analysis, highlighting the primary causes of all deviations outside established and management approved tolerances.

5-18 ITEM MASTER AND SUPPORTING DATA ACCURACY

There is a development and maintenance process in place that ensures accurate item master and supporting data. Item master and supporting data accuracy is within 95–100%.

5-19 INVENTORY RECORD ACCURACY

There is an inventory control process in place that provides accurate warehouse, stockroom, stockyard, storage tanks, and work-in-process inventory data. At least 95% of all item inventory records match physical counts within a defined counting tolerance.

5-20 BILL OF MATERIAL STRUCTURE AND ACCURACY

The planning and control process is supported by a properly structured, accurate, and integrated set of bills of material (formulas, recipes) and related data. Bill of material accuracy is within 98–100%.

5-21 ROUTING STRUCTURE AND ACCURACY

When routings are applicable, there is a development and maintenance process in place that provides accurate routing information. Routing accuracy is within 95–100%.

5-22 WORK LOCATION RECORD ACCURACY

There is a work location development and maintenance process in place that ensures accurate work location (work center, production line, work cell) data. Work location accuracy is within 95–100%.

5-23 EDUCATION AND TRAINING†

An active education and training program focused on business issues, customer issues, and operational improvements is in place for all company personnel. Its objectives include enhancing people's skills, increasing process flexibility, sharing tools/technology understanding, and meeting future needs. Education and training are viewed as a strategic advantage, and the knowledge gained is measured by its successful application to the job.

5-24 DISTRIBUTION RESOURCE PLANNING

Distribution resource planning, where applicable, is utilized to manage the logistics of distribution. Distribution requirements and resource planning information are used for sales and operations planning, master scheduling, supplier scheduling, transportation planning, warehouse planning, and shipment planning.

OVERVIEW AND DETAIL ITEMS

4—EXCELLENT   3—VERY GOOD   2—FAIR   1—POOR   0—NOT DOING

5-1 COMMITMENT TO EXCELLENCE*

□ □ □ □ □

There is a commitment by top management and throughout the company to use effective planning and control processes and tools. A single set of numbers is used by all members of the organization. These numbers represent valid plans that people believe and use to run the business

5-2 SALES AND OPERATIONS PLANNING

□ □ □ □ □

The sales and operations planning process focuses on customer requirements, supports the annual business plans, and aligns the entire organization in support of business strategy. The S&OP process is action-oriented, where management aggressively resolves problems to maintain balance between market demands and available resources.

4—EXCELLENT
3—VERY GOOD
2—FAIR
1—POOR
0—NOT DOING

5-2a   There is a concise written sales and operations planning policy that covers the process, purpose, activities, participants, and expected results. Additionally, there is a well documented procedure that details the pre-S&OP, S&OP, and post-S&OP activities. Specific roles and responsibilities are assigned, understood, and accepted.   ☐ ☐ ☐ ☐ ☐

5-2b   Sales and operations planning is truly a process, not just a monthly meeting. The process has a clear focus on intermediate to longer-term time periods; detailed product and customer issues consume little time. The process views the future on a rolling horizon basis. There is not a fixation on points such as year-end where the process becomes short sighted. One of the final steps in the process is the executive approval meeting.   ☐ ☐ ☐ ☐ ☐

5-2c   Defined activity dates are set well ahead to avoid schedule conflicts. In case the sales and operations planning regular participant is unable to attend the monthly meeting, he or she is represented by someone who is empowered to speak for the function. This also applies to emergency meetings.   ☐ ☐ ☐ ☐ ☐

4—EXCELLENT 3—VERY GOOD 2—FAIR 1—POOR 0—NOT DOING

5-2d A formal sales and operations planning
packet is circulated at least 24 hours prior
to the meeting. This packet includes the
agenda, objectives, past performance,
assumptions, product family reviews, major program updates, and minutes from the
last meeting. The agenda should clearly
identify all issues that will be raised for review and decision as a result of the pre-
S&OP process steps.

5-2e For each product family, plans are reviewed in the units of measure that communicate to all functions most effectively.

5-2f New product development as well as major
program and project schedules are reviewed
during the sales and operations planning
process. These reviews concentrate on all
major initiatives' impact on resources, revenues, and costs. Changes in launch dates,
promotions, etc. are also discussed.

4 – EXCELLENT
3 – VERY GOOD
2 – FAIR
1 – POOR
0 – NOT DOING

5-2g   All participants come prepared to the sales and operations planning meeting. There are pre-meeting activities by function that need to take place: sales and marketing to prepare a demand (sales) plan, research and development (engineers) to prepare a new product plan, operations (manufacturing) to prepare a supply (production) plan, and finance to prepare a revenue and cost plan. Corrective action plans must be developed to rebalance available resources with changes in market demand when needed.

☐ ☐ ☐ ☐ ☐

5-2h   The presentation of information includes a review of both past performances (minimum of 3 months) and future plans (typically 18 to 24 months) for: sales, production, inventory, backlog, shipments, and new product activity.

☐ ☐ ☐ ☐ ☐

5-2i   Inventory (finished goods) and/or delivery lead time (backlog) strategies are reviewed each month as part of the process.

☐ ☐ ☐ ☐ ☐

5-2j   There is a process of reviewing and documenting assumptions about the business, and reviewing the alignment in support of the business strategy. This is done to enhance the understanding of the business and represents the basis for future projections.

☐ ☐ ☐ ☐ ☐

5-2k   Sales and operations planning is an action process. Conflicts are resolved and decisions are made, documented, communicated, and implemented. Consensus is reached on a single, current operating plan.

□ □ □ □ □

5-2l   Any large and/or unanticipated changes are communicated to all functions prior to the sales and operations planning meeting. Disclosing surprises in the meeting without communicating to others is considered unacceptable behavior.

□ □ □ □ □

5-2m   Minutes of the meeting are circulated immediately after the meeting. This is typically done within twenty-four (maximum forty-eight) hours of meeting closure.

□ □ □ □ □

5-2n   The mechanism is in place to ensure that aggregate sales plans agree with detailed sales plans. There is consensus from all participants in the meeting.

□ □ □ □ □

5-2o   The mechanism is in place to ensure that aggregate operations plans agree with detailed operations plans (master schedules). There is consensus from all participants in the meeting.

□ □ □ □ □

5-2p   Rough-cut capacity planning is used to validate the reasonableness of the sales and operations plans. Required changes to these plans are made prior to release.

□ □ □ □ □

4—EXCELLENT 3—VERY GOOD 2—FAIR 1—POOR 0—NOT DOING

5-2q   The resulting sales and operations (production) plans are communicated to the master scheduling function at least monthly.

☐ ☐ ☐ ☐ ☐

5-2r   Time zones have been established as guidelines for managing changes. In the near-term, there is an effort to minimize the changes in order to gain the benefits of stability. In the mid-term range, changes are expected but are reviewed to ensure that they are realistic. In the long-term, less precision is expected but direction is established.

☐ ☐ ☐ ☐ ☐

5-2s   There is a computer-based simulation process supporting sales and operations planning that permits the evaluation of various levels of demand, supply, inventory, backlogs, projected shipments and resulting financials.

☐ ☐ ☐ ☐ ☐

5-2t   Tolerances are established to determine acceptable performance for: sales, engineering, production, and finance. These are reviewed and updated regularly. Accountability is clearly established.

☐ ☐ ☐ ☐ ☐

5-2u   The entire business is included in the sales and operations planning process. The sum of the product families can be reconciled to the revenue and profit plan.

☐ ☐ ☐ ☐ ☐

5-2v   There is an ongoing critique of the sales and operations planning process.

☐ ☐ ☐ ☐ ☐

□ □ □ □ □

5-3 FINANCIAL PLANNING, REPORTING, AND MEASUREMENT

There is a single set of numbers used by all functions within the operating environment which provides the source data used for financial planning, reporting, and measurement.

5-3a   The financial projections developed in the   □ □ □ □ □
sales and operations planning process are linked to the company's goals, strategies, and business plans. When financial projections differ from the business plan, the differences are reconciled, and either the sales and operations plan or the business plan is updated in order to ensure continuity, establish accountability, and measure performance.

5-3b   Finance uses the same source data as other   □ □ □ □ □
functions for sales, operations, shipments, and any other operating information.

5-3c   Finance recognizes the limitations of   □ □ □ □ □
traditional performance measurements, particularly those related to overhead allocation. Financial measurements, particularly those related to overhead allocation, have been reviewed and updated as necessary to support effective business practices.

5-3d   All financial systems (billing, accounts   □ □ □ □ □
payable, cost accounting), are fully integrated with all operating systems, and the information is accurate.

5-3e   Accounts payable, purchasing, and receiving systems are integrated with all material receipt transactions.

5-3f   Labor reporting, either in the form of transactions or in the form of an allocation of labor hours, is used to determine the cost of the product.

5-3g   Where work orders are used, move transactions are used to record movement of inventory from one general ledger account to another as well as to trigger variance reports for cost accounting purposes.

5-3h   All shipment transactions update the appropriate inventory and the billing system at the same time.

5-3i   Cash flow projections are prepared using the numbers from the operating system. These projections, which cover the sales and operations planning horizon, are reviewed at least monthly, and revised as changes occur.

5-3j   Simulation processes and tools are actively used to convert operating data into financial data quickly for the purpose of analysis, decision-making, and contingency planning.

5-3k   Finance is proactive in simplifying all financial processes and eliminating non-value-added activities.

5-4 ACCOUNTABLE FORECASTING PROCESS

☐ EXCELLENT ☐ VERY GOOD ☐ FAIR ☐ POOR ☐ NOT DOING

There is a process for forecasting all anticipated demands with sufficient detail and an adequate planning horizon to support business planning, sales and operations planning, and master scheduling. Forecast accuracy is measured and appropriate action taken in order to continuously improve the accuracy and forecast process.

5-4a   There is clear accountability for developing the forecast, and the importance of this effort is reflected in the organization and reporting relationship of the forecasting function.   ☐ ☐ ☐ ☐ ☐

5-4b   The forecaster (frequently called the demand manager or demand planner) understands the product, customer base, marketplace, and the company operating system.   ☐ ☐ ☐ ☐ ☐

5-4c   The demand forecast considers inputs from sales, marketing, product development, product and brand management, and business development. It considers external factors that impact demand, including economic factors, industry indicators, and competition. The demand forecast also considers time-phased forecasts and schedules communicated by customers.   ☐ ☐ ☐ ☐ ☐

4—EXCELLENT
3—VERY GOOD
2—FAIR
1—POOR
0—NOT DOING

5-4d   Available statistical forecasting tools are utilized when and where applicable. These statistical tools enable the forecaster to understand the historical baseline, trends, and seasonality of the demand; this information is used to help predict future demand.   ☐ ☐ ☐ ☐ ☐

5-4e   Spare parts, as well as other lower-level demands, are handled within the forecasting system. An appropriate order-entry mechanism that introduces firm demands at the right level in the detailed material planning process is in place.   ☐ ☐ ☐ ☐ ☐

5-4f   Forecast consumption processes are effectively used to prevent planning nervousness.   ☐ ☐ ☐ ☐ ☐

5-4g   Detailed forecasts are reconciled with aggregate forecasts and communicated to the sales force and master scheduler.   ☐ ☐ ☐ ☐ ☐

5-4h   All significant assumptions underlying the forecast are documented. They are reviewed at least monthly and updated as market conditions change.   ☐ ☐ ☐ ☐ ☐

5-4i   The forecaster participates in the product development and demand management processes.   ☐ ☐ ☐ ☐ ☐

5-4j   Aggregate and detailed forecasts are reviewed monthly during the sales premeeting process. Corrective action is taken to improve these forecasts.   ☐ ☐ ☐ ☐ ☐

4—EXCELLENT 3—VERY GOOD 2—FAIR 1—POOR 0—NOT DOING

☐ ☐ ☐ ☐ ☐

5-5 SALES PLANS

There is a formal sales planning process in place with sales and marketing responsible and accountable for developing and executing the resulting sales/bookings plan. Differences between the sales plan and actual sales are reconciled, and sales plan performance is measured.

5-5a   The sales and marketing functions understand the impact of sales planning on the company's ability to deliver the right product, in the right quantity, at the right time, thereby satisfying customers.

☐ ☐ ☐ ☐ ☐

5-5b   Actual sales are measured against sales plans. Measurements are broken down into product families and mix. Performance for sales responsibility areas is measured as well. The accuracy of these sales plans is measured and reported. Sales plan accuracy measurements are correlated to inventory turns to monitor the impact of the sales planning process on inventory.

☐ ☐ ☐ ☐ ☐

5-5c   The sales planning process is designed in such a way as to minimize the administrative impact on the sales force.

☐ ☐ ☐ ☐ ☐

5-5d   The incentives of the sales compensation system are effective and do not inject bias into the sales forecast and sales plan.

☐ ☐ ☐ ☐ ☐

4—EXCELLENT 3—VERY GOOD 2—FAIR 1—POOR 0—NOT DOING

5-5e   The sales force is actively pursuing customer linking. The customer's planning system is linked with the company's planning system to provide visibility of future demands.

☐ ☐ ☐ ☐ ☐

5-5f   Aggregate sales plans are reconciled with the mix plan. This process takes place at least monthly.

☐ ☐ ☐ ☐ ☐

5-5g   Sales participates with marketing in a demand planning session to prepare for each sales and operations planning meeting. A system is in place to communicate customer and competitor intelligence information to demand planning/forecasting.

☐ ☐ ☐ ☐ ☐

5-5h   Sales areas are provided with useful feedback regarding their performance to plan at least monthly. Sales plans are stated in terms that are meaningful to sales, yet of sufficient detail to be translated into terms which are meaningful to the supply organization and can be appropriately utilized in sales and operations planning.

☐ ☐ ☐ ☐ ☐

5-5i   The assumptions underlying the sales plan are documented. They are reviewed on a regular basis and changed as necessary.

☐ ☐ ☐ ☐ ☐

CUSTOMER PLANNING AND SATISFACTION

Customer order entry and promising are integrated with master scheduling and inventory management. There are mechanisms for matching incoming orders to forecasts, handling abnormal demands, and making sound delivery commitments based on a valid master schedule as well as accurate inventory data.

5-6a   The order promising function has access to appropriate and timely information, such as Available-to-Promise (ATP), to ensure that good promises are made. Where lead times have been reduced such that production is based on customer order receipt, order promising is based on the product family production rate. Otherwise, order promising is based on the available-to-promise for each item ordered.

☐ ☐ ☐ ☐ ☐

5-6b   Sales and marketing, along with manufacturing, participate in developing appropriate time zones/decision points for managing change.

☐ ☐ ☐ ☐ ☐

5-6c   There is a process in place for identifying and managing abnormal demands. Once identified, abnormal demand is handled according to a written policy and procedure.

☐ ☐ ☐ ☐ ☐

5-6d   Abnormal demand (both active and history) is identified properly in the company's database.

☐ ☐ ☐ ☐ ☐

5-6e   Customer orders are processed on a timely basis. The number of customer orders awaiting processing is measured and managed. ☐ ☐ ☐ ☐ ☐

5-6f   There is simulation capability used to support customer-order entry and promising in determining the effects of making unplanned customer promises. ☐ ☐ ☐ ☐ ☐

5-6g   Order-entry errors are measured and managed to eliminate the causes of the errors. ☐ ☐ ☐ ☐ ☐

5-6h   The number of customer-initiated sales change orders is measured and managed to an acceptable level. ☐ ☐ ☐ ☐ ☐

5-7 MASTER SCHEDULING   ☐ ☐ ☐ ☐ ☐
The master scheduling process is perpetually managed in order to ensure a balance of stability and responsiveness. The master schedule is reconciled monthly with the production plan resulting from the sales and operations planning process.

5-7a   Accountability for maintaining a valid master schedule is clear. The importance of master scheduling is reflected in the organization and reporting relationship within the company. ☐ ☐ ☐ ☐ ☐

5-7b   The master scheduler (supply manager) understands the product, manufacturing process, and purchasing process, as well as the planning and control system. ☐ ☐ ☐ ☐ ☐

5-7c   A formal job description exists that details
the responsibilities and performance measurements for the master scheduling/
supply management function.

☐ ☐ ☐ ☐ ☐

5-7d   The master scheduler participates in and
provides important detail information to
the sales and operations planning process.

☐ ☐ ☐ ☐

5-7e   The master scheduler responds to feedback
that identifies areas where the master schedule impacts material and/or capacity availability by initiating problem-resolution
action.

☐ ☐ ☐ ☐ ☐

5-7f   The master scheduler has empathy for customers, sales, and marketing while being
sensitive to manufacturing and supplier
objectives and constraints.

☐ ☐ ☐ ☐ ☐

5-7g   The master schedule takes into account all
demands, including forecasts, contracts,
customer orders, samples, specials, proto-
types, spares, interplant, etc. The master
schedule directs and drives all manufacturing, purchasing, and manufacturing-
related engineering activities.

☐ ☐ ☐ ☐ ☐

4—EXCELLENT 3—VERY GOOD 2—FAIR 1—POOR 0—NOT DOING

5-7h   The master scheduler is notified of all ab- ☐ ☐ ☐ ☐ ☐
         normal demand entering the planning and
         control system. Since abnormal demand
         may be incremental to the expected de-
         mand, appropriate action is taken to ensure
         total customer satisfaction and support the
         business strategy, not just identification of
         the abnormal demand order.

5-7i   The system has a Firm Planned Order ☐ ☐ ☐ ☐ ☐
         (FPO) capability that is used to take control
         of the master schedule covering the horizon
         within the Planning Time Fence (PTF).

5-7j   A formal process is in place that defines how ☐ ☐ ☐ ☐ ☐
         planning bills (if appropriate) are used to
         plan material and capacity as well as to di-
         rect the finishing/final assembly operations.

5-7k   Planning bills of material (if used) are main- ☐ ☐ ☐ ☐ ☐
         tained jointly by master scheduling, de-
         mand management, sales, and marketing.

5-7l   A written master schedule policy is ☐ ☐ ☐ ☐ ☐
         followed to monitor stability and respon-
         siveness; goals are established and perfor-
         mance is measured.

5-7m   The master schedule is "firmed up" over a ☐ ☐ ☐ ☐ ☐
         sufficient horizon to enable stability of op-
         erations. Guidelines for this firmed hori-
         zon include: cumulative material and
         manufacturing lead time, lead time to plan
         and adjust capacity, and lead time to es-
         tablish and maintain supplier agreements.

4—EXCELLENT 3—VERY GOOD 2—FAIR 1—POOR 0—NOT DOING

5-7n   Master schedule changes within the planning time zones are managed; changes are authorized by the appropriate people, measured, and reviewed for cause.   ☐ ☐ ☐ ☐ ☐

5-7o   Policies govern the use of safety stock and/or option overplanning when used to increase responsiveness and compensate for inconsistent supply and/or demand variations.   ☐ ☐ ☐ ☐ ☐

5-7p   Available-to-Promise (ATP) information is monitored for completeness and accuracy. The use of ATP is governed by a written policy and not violated except when approved by top management.   ☐ ☐ ☐ ☐ ☐

5-7q   The master schedule is summarized appropriately and reconciled with the agreed-to production rate (production plan) from the sales and operations planning process.   ☐ ☐ ☐ ☐ ☐

5-7r   No items on the master schedule are past due. The master scheduler, and other affected company personnel recognize an item cannot be manufactured, purchased, or shipped in past time periods.   ☐ ☐ ☐ ☐ ☐

5-7s   All master schedule exception–driven action messages are reviewed, analyzed, and acted upon at least weekly.   ☐ ☐ ☐ ☐ ☐

5-7t   The master schedule is expressed in weekly, daily, or smaller time periods. It may be work order– or rate-based and is replanned at least weekly.   ☐ ☐ ☐ ☐ ☐

4—EXCELLENT   3—VERY GOOD   2—FAIR   1—POOR   0—NOT DOING

5-7u   There is a defined process to determine   ☐ ☐ ☐ ☐ ☐
what levels in the product structure are to be
master scheduled. Criteria such as customer expected lead times, competition's
quoted lead times, willingness to invest in
inventory, willingness to invest in capacity,
desired production flexibility, priority control, and marketplace demands are all taken
into account during the selection process.

5-7v   The alternative approaches used with   ☐ ☐ ☐ ☐ ☐
planning bills to develop option and production forecasts for master scheduled
items are well understood and an appropriate process is used to maintain them.

5-7w   Rough-cut capacity planning, or its equiv-   ☐ ☐ ☐ ☐ ☐
alent, is used to evaluate the impact of
significant master schedule changes on
critical resources. Planned capacity is compared to required capacity and appropriate
adjustments are made to ensure a balanced
capacity plan and master schedule.

5-7x   A finishing/final assembly mechanism or   ☐ ☐ ☐ ☐ ☐
kanban approach is integrated with the
master schedule to ensure orderly transi-
tion from planning to execution (control).
The finishing process guides customer orders or finished goods replenishments to
completion.

	4—EXCELLENT	3—VERY GOOD	2—FAIR	1—POOR	0—NOT DOING

5-7y   A weekly master schedule communications meeting exists and is attended by all affected functions.   □ □ □ □ □

5-7z   When applicable, the linearity or levelness of output is measured; the graphic illustration of results should reflect weekly or daily performance to a planned linear output; reasons for deviations are highlighted with appropriate analysis.   □ □ □ □ □

5-8 MATERIAL PLANNING AND CONTROL   □ □ □ □ □
There is a material planning process that maintains valid material plans along with a control process that communicates priorities through production schedules, supplier schedules, and/or kanban mechanisms.

5-8a   Material planners and schedulers understand the product, manufacturing process, and purchasing process, as well as a manufacturing planning and control system. Accountability for creating and maintaining a valid plan for material is assigned, understood, and accepted.   □ □ □ □ □

5-8b   All involved personnel, including material planning, production, and purchasing, operate under the "silence is approval" principle and are responsible to advise of schedule-adherence problems that cannot be resolved to the appropriate function.   □ □ □ □ □

4—EXCELLENT   3—VERY GOOD   2—FAIR   1—POOR   0—NOT DOING

5-8c   Material planners are responsible for creating, maintaining, reviewing, and analyzing the validity of all appropriate planning parameters such as order quantities, lot sizes, lead times, scrap factors, shrinkage, safety stocks, etc.   □ □ □ □ □

5-8d   Production and purchasing understand and use the planning and control system. Accountability for maintaining valid data under their responsibility is assigned, understood, and accepted. Material plan audits are conducted monthly, and the audits reflect plan validity to be in the 95–100% range.   □ □ □ □ □

5-8e   There are formal communication processes among material planning, production, and purchasing for the purpose of exchanging information needed to maintain valid material plans and schedules. The frequency and format (meetings, reports, electronic mail) are determined by the situation.   □ □ □ □ □

5-8f   The informal priority systems (shortage list, hot list, priority codes, etc.) have been eliminated, and there is only one formalized priority-setting mechanism.   □ □ □ □ □

5-8g   Material plans are expressed in weekly or smaller time periods to provide appropriate resolution of priorities.   □ □ □ □ □

4—EXCELLENT 3—VERY GOOD 2—FAIR 1—POOR 0—NOT DOING

5-8h   The material planning system is run as frequently as required to maintain valid
schedules. Daily may be required, but
weekly processing is a minimum.

5-8i   The system uses industry accepted stan-
dard logic to generate exception-driven ac-
tion messages, including Need to Release
Order, Need to Reschedule Order, Need to
Cancel Order, Past Due, or Release Past
Due.

5-8j   The system has a firm planned order capability that is used, when necessary, to override the suggested plan.

5-8k   Material planners understand bottom-up
replanning using single-level pegging to
reconcile problems. The firm planned order system capability is used as needed to
maintain valid plans.

5-8l   The system has an effective component
availability checking mechanism that material planners use to determine the feasi-
bility of releasing production orders or
schedules.

5-8m   The system includes the capability to alter
the bill of material for individual orders
and jobs.

5-8n   All exception-driven action messages are
prioritized, reviewed, and resolved in a
timely manner.

5-8o   The number of exception-driven action messages for each material planner is monitored for activity, trends, and volume. This data is used to ensure the necessary work is getting done and enough planner capacity exists to handle all the action messages.

5-8p   Where work orders are used, the volume of reschedules is tracked to monitor the stability of the plan and to determine the causes of excessive rescheduling activity.

5-8q   Where work orders are used, orders are released with full material availability and full lead time 95–100% of the time.

5-9 SUPPLIER PLANNING AND CONTROL
A supplier planning and scheduling process provides visibility for key items over an adequate planning horizon. A supply management process exists that ensures effective control of the established supply chain.

5-9a   Suppliers that represent at least 80% of the dollar volume for purchased material have been educated in material planning principles and understand the supplier scheduling process.

5-9b   Where appropriate, traditional purchase orders have been replaced by long-term supplier agreements.

4—EXCELLENT
3—VERY GOOD
2—FAIR
1—POOR
0—NOT DOING

5-9c   Suppliers agree to plan raw material and capacity to meet the requirements displayed on the supplier schedule.

5-9d   There is a clear policy defining supplier scheduler and buyer responsibilities, including at what point each becomes involved in problem resolution.

5-9e   Supplier agreements are in place for all suppliers participating in the company's supplier scheduling program. These agreements are periodically reviewed to ensure completeness and validity. Accountability for maintaining these agreements is assigned, understood, and accepted.

5-9f   The supplier schedule displays planned orders as well as scheduled receipts over the planning horizon for all items provided by the supplier.

5-9g   Commitment zones are established in the supplier schedule representing firm commitments, material commitments, and capacity planning commitments.

5-9h   Time periods on the supplier schedule are weeks or smaller for at least the firm commitment zone.

5-9i   The supplier scheduler and/or buyers meet with production planners as frequently as required to maintain a valid schedule.

4—EXCELLENT 3—VERY GOOD 2—FAIR 1—POOR 0—NOT DOING

5-9j   The suppliers understand the principle be- ☐ ☐ ☐ ☐ ☐
hind "silence is approval" and agree to no-
tify the buyer in advance if a due date will
be missed.

5-9k   Supplier schedules are communicated to ☐ ☐ ☐ ☐ ☐
suppliers at least weekly.

5-9l   For nonsupplier scheduled items, 95% of ☐ ☐ ☐ ☐ ☐
purchase orders are released with full lead
time.

5-9m   There is a purchasing policy that states the ☐ ☐ ☐ ☐ ☐
set of criteria that defines the items which
are planned and scheduled through the
supplier scheduling process.

5-10 CAPACITY PLANNING AND CONTROL ☐ ☐ ☐ ☐ ☐
*There is a capacity planning process using rough-
cut capacity planning and, where applicable,
capacity requirements planning in which planned
capacity, based on demonstrated output, is balanced
with required capacity. A capacity control process
is used to measure and manage manufacturing
requirements, work throughput, and queue levels.*

5-10a Capacity planning is well understood by ☐ ☐ ☐ ☐ ☐
all appropriate personnel and used to plan
labor and equipment requirements.

4—EXCELLENT 3—VERY GOOD 2—FAIR 1—POOR 0—NOT DOING

5-10b   There is an understanding of the respective responsibilities of the capacity planner (scheduling) and production (manufacturing) in the capacity management process. Accountability for maintaining the accuracy of schedules and production-oriented planning data, such as planned capacity, number of workers, number of machines, and number of shifts, is assigned, understood, and accepted.

5-10c   Production and capacity planners meet at least weekly to resolve capacity issues.

5-10d   All activities that consume capacity are considered in identifying capacity requirements (e.g., maintenance, engineering projects, specials, etc.).

5-10e   When necessary, other constraints such as engineering and suppliers' capacity are considered in the capacity management process.

5-10f   Work areas are appropriately defined to enable control of priorities and capacities while minimizing data maintenance, transactions, and reports.

5-10g   A "Load Factor" that recognizes capacity loss due to efficiency, utilization, absenteeism, meetings, and anything else that is not included in the proper application of standard times is maintained and used in projecting capacity.

4—EXCELLENT 3—VERY GOOD 2—FAIR 1—POOR 0—NOT DOING

5-10h   Demonstrated capacity is measured and used to update planned capacity (demonstrated capacity plus or minus any planned capacity changes). □ □ □ □ □

5-10i   Corrective action is taken to reschedule overdue capacity requirements caused by past due orders. □ □ □ □ □

5-10j   The capacity planning process includes appropriate analysis of the elements that make up demonstrated capacity such as efficiency, utilization, absenteeism, etc. □ □ □ □ □

5-10k   Where applicable, capacity requirements planning is used to evaluate detailed capacity constraints when planning and identifying labor and equipment needs. □ □ □ □ □

5-10l   Capacity detail and summary screens or reports by work area are available in a graphic or matrix format and used by capacity planners to identify capacity and scheduling problems. □ □ □ □ □

5-10m   There is a process in place that includes variance analysis of work area planned and actual input, output, and queue levels. □ □ □ □ □

4—EXCELLENT 3—VERY GOOD 2—FAIR 1—POOR 0—NOT DOING

☐ ☐ ☐ ☐ ☐

5-11 PRODUCTION PLANNING AND CONTROL

There is a planning process supported by a control process that creates, maintains, and synchronizes detailed production schedules. These synchronized schedules communicate valid manufacturing priorities through various methods to the shop floor.

5-11a Production is accountable to meet scheduled operation due dates, daily run rates, kanban replenishments, etc. in a timely manner.

☐ ☐ ☐ ☐ ☐

5-11b Production understands the product, manufacturing process, and priority scheduling mechanisms being used.

☐ ☐ ☐ ☐ ☐

5-11c Process instructions are readily available for the various operations needed to build the product.

☐ ☐ ☐ ☐ ☐

5-11d A formal job description exists that details the responsibilities and performance measurements for the production function.

☐ ☐ ☐ ☐ ☐

5-11e Production works to a formal schedule that is communicated through various methods.

☐ ☐ ☐ ☐ ☐

5-11f The informal priority system, i.e., the hot list, has been eliminated. Emergency phone calls, expedite meetings, hot stickers, etc. are not honored in production.

☐ ☐ ☐ ☐ ☐

4—EXCELLENT 3—VERY GOOD 2—FAIR 1—POOR 0—NOT DOING

5-11g   The production floor is orderly, clean, and lacks clutter. Production flows in a uniform manner as defined in production policies and procedures.

☐ ☐ ☐ ☐ ☐

5-11h   Production personnel have been educated and trained in using the output from the planning and control system. Regularly scheduled training classes are held to ensure cross training of production personnel in multiple skills and work areas.

☐ ☐ ☐ ☐ ☐

5-11i   Production is responsible for feeding back all potential production problems to the master scheduler if these problems affect the company's ability to meet the master schedule.

☐ ☐ ☐ ☐ ☐

5-11j   The planning and control process includes a capability to display production schedules on a daily basis. These schedules are shown on computer screens, reports, boards, graphs, etc.

☐ ☐ ☐ ☐ ☐

5-11k   The production schedules are expressed in weekly, daily, or smaller time periods. These schedules may be work order– or rate-based and are replanned daily (maximum weekly).

☐ ☐ ☐ ☐ ☐

5-11l   The planning and control process includes a capability to modify or override any system-created start or completion date.

☐ ☐ ☐ ☐ ☐

	4—EXCELLENT	3—VERY GOOD	2—FAIR	1—POOR	0—NOT DOING

5-11m   The planning and control process includes the capability to report work status by operation or kanban replenishment cycle.   ☐ ☐ ☐ ☐ ☐

5-11n   An anticipated delay reporting process is used to inform need-to-know functions of lateness of work and correction action being taken.   ☐ ☐ ☐ ☐ ☐

5-11o   Regularly (daily or weekly) production meetings are held to ensure that everyone in production understands the work priorities. These formal meetings are conducted using agendas and common schedules (single set of numbers).   ☐ ☐ ☐ ☐ ☐

5-11p   Point-of-usage inventory in production is managed using formal inventory management principles. Inventory record accuracy measurements and cycle counting procedures are used in production much like they are used in the stockroom.   ☐ ☐ ☐ ☐ ☐

The following items are key performance measurements of planning and control processes. See Appendix A for the preferred method of calculating the following performance measurements; see Appendix B for supplemental measurements.

5-12 CUSTOMER SERVICE   ☐ ☐ ☐ ☐ ☐

An objective for on-time deliveries exists and customers are in agreement with it. Performance against the objective is measured and results confirm that performance to defined fill rates and/or promised delivery dates is 95–100%. Graphs or charts showing actual performance versus plan are maintained along with the appropriate analysis, highlighting the primary causes of all deviations outside established and management tolerances.

5-13 SALES PLAN PERFORMANCE*   ☐ ☐ ☐ ☐ ☐

Accountability is established by measuring sales performance to plan. Sales plans are directly aligned to support the S&OP process. Performance metrics for sales plan performance are in alignment with other operating metrics. Graphs or charts showing actual performance versus plan are maintained along with the appropriate analysis, highlighting the primary causes of all deviations outside established and management tolerances.

5-14 PRODUCTION PLAN PERFORMANCE*

Accountability for production plan performance has been established, and the goals and method of measurement agreed upon. All goals, metrics, and performance results are communicated to appropriate company functions. Production plan performance is within ±2% of the monthly plan by product family, except in produce-to-order environments when demand is less than plan. In this case the performance is within ±2% of the demand. If a change in the production plan is authorized by top management, the measure is made against the newly authorized plan. Graphs or charts showing actual performance versus plan are maintained along with the appropriate analysis, highlighting the primary causes of all deviations outside established and management approved tolerances.

5-15 MASTER SCHEDULE PERFORMANCE*

Accountability for master schedule performance has been established, and the goals and method of measurement agreed upon. All goals, metrics, and performance results are communicated to appropriate company functions. Master schedule performance is 95–100% of the plan. Graphs or charts showing actual performance versus plan are maintained along with the appropriate analysis, highlighting the primary causes of all deviations outside established and management approved tolerances.

5-16 MANUFACTURING SCHEDULE PERFORMANCE*

Accountability for manufacturing schedule performance has been established, and the goals and method of measurement agreed upon. All goals, metrics, and performance results are communicated to appropriate company functions. Manufacturing schedule performance is 95–100% of the plan. Graphs or charts showing actual performance versus plan are maintained along with the appropriate analysis, highlighting the primary causes of all deviations outside established and management approved tolerances.

5-17 SUPPLIER DELIVERY PERFORMANCE*

Accountability for supplier delivery performance has been established, and the goals and method of measurement agreed upon. All goals, metrics, and performance results are communicated to appropriate company functions. Supplier delivery performance is 95–100% of the plan. Graphs or charts showing actual performance versus plan are maintained along with the appropriate analysis, highlighting the primary causes of all deviations outside established and management approved tolerances.

5-18 ITEM MASTER AND SUPPORTING DATA ACCURACY

There is a development and maintenance process in place that ensures accurate item master and supporting data. Item master and supporting data accuracy is within 95–100%.

	4—EXCELLENT	3—VERY GOOD	2—FAIR	1—POOR	0—NOT DOING

5-18a Accountability for creating and maintaining accurate item master and supporting data is clearly understood by those with item master and supporting data input responsibility. Examples of item master data include item identification, description, units of measure, lead times, lot sizes, costs, etc. Supporting data may be interpreted as that data contained in customer, supplier, and company records.

□ □ □ □ □

5-18b Review and audit procedures are used to identify and resolve data file errors. The process examines, at a minimum, item number, description, units of measure, planning lead times, lot sizes, order quantities, make/buy designator, and time fences. This process is also used to measure item record accuracy.

□ □ □ □ □

5-18c The review and audit process is conducted on a monthly (minimum) basis. The number of records audited each month should be statistically sound (or at least 30) and based upon the company's total number of item master records. Supporting data records are also reviewed periodically.

□ □ □ □ □

5-18d Problem root-cause analysis is practiced to eliminate the underlying cause of errors.

□ □ □ □ □

4—EXCELLENT 3—VERY GOOD 2—FAIR 1—POOR 0—NOT DOING

5-18e   Monthly audit results show the database record accuracy to be a minimum of 95% (95 out of every 100 items examined require no significant adjustments).

☐ ☐ ☐ ☐ ☐

5-19 INVENTORY RECORD ACCURACY

☐ ☐ ☐ ☐ ☐

There is an inventory control process in place that provides accurate warehouse, stockroom, stockyard, storage tanks, and work-in-process inventory data. At least 95% of all item inventory records match physical counts within a defined counting tolerance.

5-19a   There is a written policy that clearly identifies responsibility and accountability for maintaining accurate inventory records. This policy is clearly understood by all people controlling inventories and includes product-related inventory.

☐ ☐ ☐ ☐ ☐

5-19b   Cycle counting is done on a daily (minimum weekly) basis. The number of records audited each week should be statistically sound (or at least 30) and based upon the company's total number of inventory records.

☐ ☐ ☐ ☐ ☐

5-19c   Daily or weekly cycle counting procedures are used to identify and resolve inventory errors. Additionally, these procedures are used to measure inventory accuracy.

☐ ☐ ☐ ☐ ☐

5-19d   The cycle counting process has replaced the monthly and annual physical inventory.

☐ ☐ ☐ ☐ ☐

4—EXCELLENT 3—VERY GOOD 2—FAIR 1—POOR 0—NOT DOING

5-19e   Cycle count results show sustained inventory record accuracy to be 95–100%.   ☐ ☐ ☐ ☐ ☐

5-19f   There is a policy that states all inventory-related transactions are processed at least daily to update the inventory management system. Audits are periodically conducted to ensure the policy is being followed and inventory transactions are posted accurately.   ☐ ☐ ☐ ☐ ☐

5-19g   When backflush or post (automatic) deduct is used in point-of-use/floor stock situations, the following rules are observed: ☐ ☐ ☐ ☐ ☐

- Bills of material, recipes, and formulas must be 99% accurate.
- All scrap is properly reported.
- All substitutes are properly documented.
- Actual (usage) locations are used.
- Production is correctly reported.
- There isn't any major delay between the usage of material and production reporting.

5-20 BILL OF MATERIAL STRUCTURE AND ACCURACY

☐ ☐ ☐ ☐ ☐

The planning and controll process is supported by a properly structured, accurate, and integrated set of bills of material (formulas, recipes) and related data. Bill of material accuracy is within 98–100%.

4—EXCELLENT 3—VERY GOOD 2—FAIR 1—POOR 0—NOT DOING

5-20a   Responsibility and accountability for developing and maintaining bills of material, recipes, and formulas are clearly defined in a written policy.

☐ ☐ ☐ ☐ ☐

5-20b   All functions that use the bills of materials, recipes, and formulas participate in their structuring.

☐ ☐ ☐ ☐ ☐

5-20c   Bills of material, recipes, and formulas are properly structured, represent the way products are produced, and support the planning and control processes.

☐ ☐ ☐ ☐ ☐

5-20d   There is a bill of material, recipe, and formula accuracy audit process in place. This process examines the bill of material at a single level, looking for all correct items and materials, quantity per, and unit of measure. The audit reviews engineering/ manufacturing bills of material and compares them to actual production of product. All must be consistent to be considered accurate. The number of bill of materials audited each week should be statistically sound (or at least 30) and based upon the company's total number of bill of materials.

☐ ☐ ☐ ☐ ☐

5-20e   Audit results show the bills of material, recipes, and formulas to be 98–100% accurate.

☐ ☐ ☐ ☐ ☐

5-20f   Finance uses the bill of material, recipe, and formula in costing the product.

☐ ☐ ☐ ☐ ☐

4—EXCELLENT 3—VERY GOOD 2—FAIR 1—POOR 0—NOT DOING

5-20g   Manufacturing uses the bills of material, recipes, or formulas to plan and control materials. □ □ □ □ □

5-20h   There is a policy and procedure in place that identifies who is responsible for creating and maintaining each element of the bill of material, recipe, or formula. This policy and procedure also identifies accountability for the accuracy of this database. □ □ □ □ □

5-21 ROUTING STRUCTURE AND ACCURACY

□ □ □ □ □

When routings are applicable, there is a development and maintenance process in place that provides accurate routing information. Routing accuracy is within 95–100%.

5-21a   There is a written policy that clearly identifies responsibility and accountability for developing and maintaining routings. □ □ □ □ □

5-21b   All functions that use the routings participate in their development. □ □ □ □ □

5-21c   The routings represent the way products are made and are integrated with the bills of material. □ □ □ □ □

4—EXCELLENT   3—VERY GOOD   2—FAIR   1—POOR   0—NOT DOING

5-21d   There is a routing accuracy audit process in place. The number or records audited each month should be statistically sound (or at least 30) and based upon the company's total number of routings. This process examines the routings for proper sequence of operations, work location, missing or unnecessary operations, set-up times, and run times (acceptable maximum tolerance is ±20% to demonstrated, and the times are consistent with one another). The audit process compares routing documentation to actual production used to make the product.   ☐ ☐ ☐ ☐ ☐

5-21e   Audit results show routings to be 95–100% accurate.   ☐ ☐ ☐ ☐ ☐

5-21f   Finance uses the routings in estimating, bidding, and costing the product.   ☐ ☐ ☐ ☐ ☐

5-21g   Manufacturing uses the routings to plan work as well as to control work.   ☐ ☐ ☐ ☐ ☐

5-21h   There is a policy and procedure in place that identifies the responsibility for creating and maintaining each element of the routing. This policy and procedure also identifies accountability for the accuracy of the routing data base.   ☐ ☐ ☐ ☐ ☐

	4—EXCELLENT	3—VERY GOOD	2—FAIR	1—POOR	0—NOT DOING

5-22 WORK LOCATION RECORD ACCURACY

There is a work location development and maintenance process in place that ensures accurate work location (work center, production line, work cell) data. Work location accuracy is within 95–100%.

5-22a   Accountability for creating and maintaining accurate work location records is clearly understood by all those controlling work areas. Examples of work areas include fabrication, sub-assembly, final assembly, mixing, blending, finishing, rework, testing, engineering, etc.

5-22b   Review and audit procedures are used to identify and resolve work location errors. The process examines, at a minimum, work location identification, equipment capacity, labor capacity, productivity (load) factors, and key parameters used by finite and infinite capacity scheduling systems.

5-22c   The review and audit process is conducted on a monthly basis. The number of records audited each month should be statistically sound (or at least 30) and based upon the company's total number of work centers.

5-22d   Problem root-cause analysis is practiced to eliminate the underlying cause of errors.

4—EXCELLENT 3—VERY GOOD 2—FAIR 1—POOR 0—NOT DOING

5-22e   Monthly audit results show the work location database to be 95–100% accurate.

□ □ □ □ □

5-23 EDUCATION AND TRAINING†

□ □ □ □ □

An active education and training program focused on business issues, customer issues, and operational improvements is in place for all company personnel. Its objectives include enhancing people's skills, increasing process flexibility, sharing tools/ technology understanding, and meeting future needs. Education and training are viewed as a strategic advantage, and the knowledge gained is measured by its successful application to the job.

5-23a   Management views education and training as a strategic advantage, and their attitude and actions demonstrate commitment and involvement to educate and train all necessary people fully prior to implementation of new processes and tools/technologies.

□ □ □ □ □

5-23b   Education and training are aligned with the strategic initiatives to assure the right education and training is done and that it is cost effective.

□ □ □ □ □

5-23c   Education is a participative process flowing in two directions (top to bottom and bottom to top) of the organization.

□ □ □ □ □

4—EXCELLENT 3—VERY GOOD 2—FAIR 1—POOR 0—NOT DOING

5-23d   The education and training program recognizes people at all levels as experts in
their respective areas. The education program uses these people to communicate
company goals and objectives, facilitate
the required change process, and measure
performance results.

5-23e   The education and training approach is
based on the principles of process and behavior change in an organization rather
than merely on fact-transfer regarding
specific tools or technologies.

5-23f   All education and training sessions clearly
define the skills needed for each job, set the
expectation that behavior will change, provide a process to assure that those skills are
acquired, and hold supervisors/leaders accountable for administering the process.

5-23g   The supervisor/leaders and employee performance evaluations are tied to successful
application of the knowledge gained in the
education and training sessions to the job.

5-23h   The company has committed adequate resources, time, and finances to education
and training.

4—EXCELLENT   3—VERY GOOD   2—FAIR   1—POOR   0—NOT DOING

5-23i   An ongoing education and training program is used to refine and improve the use of business tools such as team-based technologies, integrated business planning processes, software, etc.

☐ ☐ ☐ ☐ ☐

5-23j   Periodically, the company education and training schedule is updated and published. This education schedule includes sessions covering company policies/procedures, business processes, hardware/software, skill improvement, safety, health, environment, etc.

☐ ☐ ☐ ☐ ☐

5-23k   Areas of people improvement needs are continuously assessed.

☐ ☐ ☐ ☐ ☐

5-23l   Company personnel records are updated upon completion of education and training events.

☐ ☐ ☐ ☐ ☐

5-23m   A reference library containing published materials, education videos, computer-aided instruction disks, reference manuals, video support materials, etc., is in place to assist people in their skill development. Policies and procedures are implemented to ensure availability and maintenance of library materials.

☐ ☐ ☐ ☐ ☐

5-24 DISTRIBUTION RESOURCE PLANNING

Distribution resource planning, where applicable, is utilized to manage the logistics of distribution. Distribution requirements and resource planning information are used for sales and operations planning, master scheduling, supplier scheduling, transportation planning, warehouse planning, and shipment planning.

5-24a There is a concise, written Distribution Resource Planning policy that covers purpose, process, participants, and expected results.

5-24b Distribution requirements are considered and reconciled through the sales and operations planning and master scheduling processes.

5-24c The distribution network maintained in the distribution resource planning system is complete; it reflects which items are stocked at each distribution center.

5-24d Forecasts are available for each stockkeeping unit in each distribution center.

5-24e Time periods for distribution resource planning are weeks or smaller.

5-24f The distribution resource planning system is run at least weekly (more frequently if required).

4—EXCELLENT
3—VERY GOOD
2—FAIR
1—POOR
0—NOT DOING

5-24g   The distribution resource planning system includes necessary functions to effectively manage a distribution network and/or distribution center. Some of these functions are firm planned orders, pegging, available-to-promise, exception-driven action messages, forecasts, customer orders, etc. Additionally, the system has the capability to maintain and change inventory records, location records, and scheduled receipts.   ☐ ☐ ☐ ☐ ☐

5-24h   Distribution resource planning is utilized to evaluate planning factors (lot sizes, safety stock, lead time, etc.) and the resulting impact on inventory levels.   ☐ ☐ ☐ ☐ ☐

5-24i   The distribution resource planning process and system is integrated with an effective supplier scheduling process and system in order to provide adequate visibility to outside suppliers.   ☐ ☐ ☐ ☐ ☐

5-24j   The system provides pertinent information for transportation planning in order to be responsive to the needs of the distribution centers as well as to reduce transportation costs.   ☐ ☐ ☐ ☐ ☐

5-24k   The system provides a shipping schedule that enables cost reductions while, at the same time, satisfying established loading and shipping needs.   ☐ ☐ ☐ ☐ ☐

4—EXCELLENT 3—VERY GOOD 2—FAIR 1—POOR 0—NOT DOING

5-24l   The system provides pertinent information □ □ □ □ □
for warehouse and storage location plan-
ning in order to be responsive to the needs
of the distribution centers as well as to reduce storage costs.

5-24m   Where applicable, kanbans are used to □ □ □ □ □
trigger replenishment from a central
supply facility to the distribution centers.

Appendix A
RECOMMENDED FORMULAS

Over the years, companies have come to us after spending a great deal of time and energy on the best way to calculate the performance measures mentioned in the checklist. For this reason, we have listed the recommended formulas for these calculations in this appendix.

Sales Plan Performance by Family =

$$\frac{\text{Actual units sold for month}}{\text{Planned sales for month}} \times 100$$

*This measurement should be done at each S&OP time zone.

Sales Plan Performance by Product or Item =

$$\frac{\text{Actual units sold for month}}{\text{Planned sales for month}} \times 100$$

*This measurement should be done at each MPS time zone.

Customer Delivery Performance =

$$\frac{\text{Number of items shipped on time}}{\text{(within quantity and time tolerance)}} \times 100$$
$$\frac{\text{Number of items due to ship}}{\text{(as of original promise date)}}$$

Quality (Parts per Million/Defects per Million Parts*) =

$$\frac{\text{Defects} \times 1,000,000}{\text{Units processed*}}$$

*Could be shipments, documents, operations, etc.

Manufacturing Cost* =

$$\frac{\text{Annualized cost of goods sold}}{\text{Monthly manufacturing expense} - \text{material purchases}}$$

*Can also use for department or company.

Measures of Velocity =

$$\frac{\text{Value-added time}}{\text{Cycle time}}$$

Engineering Schedule Performance (Product Development Activity) =

$$\frac{\text{Number of deliverable milestones completed on time}}{\text{(within quality and time tolerance)}} \times 100$$
$$\frac{}{\text{Number of deliverable milestones due* during the time period}} \times 100$$

*User may define time period (week, month, etc.).

Production Plan Performance =

$$\frac{\text{Actual production for product family*} \atop \text{(this month)}}{\text{Planned production for product family*} \atop \text{(planned last month for this month)}} \times 100$$

*Can be units or a capacity unit of measure such as hours, tons, etc.
Note: With multiple product families, use a weighted average of the families.

Master Schedule Performance =

$$\frac{\text{Number of orders/schedules* completed on time} \atop \text{(within quantity and time allowance)}}{\text{Number of orders/schedules due* during the time period}} \times 100$$

*Needs interpretation when scheduling pseudo's. User may define time period (day, week, etc.).

Manufacturing Schedule Performance =

$$\frac{\text{Number of orders/schedules completed on time} \atop \text{(within quantity and time tolerance)}}{\text{Number of orders/schedules due* during the time period}} \times 100$$

*User may define time period (day, week, etc.).

Supplier Delivery Performance =

$$\frac{\text{Number of orders/schedules received on time} \atop \text{(within quantity and time tolerance)}}{\text{Number of orders/schedules due* during the time period}} \times 100$$

*User may define time period (day, week, etc.).

Item Master Accuracy =

$$\frac{\text{Number of correct item masters*}}{\text{Total number of item masters checked}} \times 100$$

*Auditing item masters identification, description, planning lead times, etc.

Supporting Data Accuracy =

$$\frac{\text{Number of correct supporting data records*}}{\text{Total number of supporting data records checked}} \times 100$$

*Auditing supporting data contained in customer, supplier, and company records.

Inventory Record Accuracy =

$$\frac{\begin{array}{c}\text{Number of correct items/quantities/locations*}\\ \text{(within quantity tolerance)}\end{array}}{\text{Number of items/quantities/locations* checked}} \times 100$$

*If discrete location identification is not required, delete from equation.

Bill of Material Accuracy =

$$\frac{\text{Number of correct bills*}}{\text{Total number of bills checked}} \times 100$$

*Auditing single-level parent number/all component relationships, quantity per, and units of measure.

Routing Accuracy =

$$\frac{\text{Number of correct routings*}}{\text{Total number of routings checked}} \times 100$$

*Auditing work-center identification, sequence of operations, and standards (within tolerance).

Master Schedule Accuracy =

$$\frac{\text{Number of valid* master schedules}}{\text{Number of master schedules checked}} \times 100$$

Valid means the due date is balanced with the need date, and the capacity plan is realistic. Reasonable tolerances for quantity and time are acceptable but must be documented.

Material Plan Accuracy =

$$\frac{\text{Number of valid* material plans}}{\text{Number of material plans checked}} \times 100$$

Valid means the due date is balanced with the need date, and the capacity plan is realistic. Reasonable tolerances for quantity and time are acceptable but must be documented.

Capacity Plan Accuracy =

$$\frac{\text{Number of valid* capacity plans}}{\text{Number of capacity plans checked}} \times 100$$

Valid means the planned capacity is balanced with the required capacity, and the material plan is doable. Reasonable tolerances for quantity and time are acceptable but must be documented.

Appendix B
EXAMPLES OF SUPPLEMENTARY PERFORMANCE MEASUREMENTS FOR PLANNING AND CONTROL PROCESSES

In a number of situations, companies have tracked some additional measurements as a way to assess the effectiveness of a particular business function. These supplementary measurements are helpful indicators in assessing how well a particular business function is being accomplished.

SALES AND OPERATIONS PLANNING

1. Sales Plan (actual vs. plan, by family, by month, etc.)
2. Production Plan (actual vs. plan, by family, by month, etc.)
3. Inventory (by product line, finished goods, raw material, work-in-process; by actual dollar level and/or turnover rate vs. current shipment plans, etc.)
4. Customer Service (backorder levels, delivery lead time, number of weeks aging of overdue customer orders, number of involuntary reschedules of customer orders, by product line, etc.)

SALES PLANNING

1. Item accuracy (by week or by month, within preestablished tolerances, by product family, by geographic region, by responsible
   Sales/Marketing personnel)
2. Family accuracy (within preestablished tolerances, by week or by
   month, by geographic region, market segment, etc.)

SALES ORDER ENTRY

1. Administrative customer-order promising time (order entry, credit
   check, document generation, and delivery, etc.)
2. Shipment processing time (custom packaging, crating, loading,
   shipping, etc.)
3. Percent sales order changes
4. Order-entry accuracy (percentage of orders entered without errors)

MASTER PRODUCTION SCHEDULING

1. Past due (percentage of current output rate, percentage of current
   in-process aging, etc.)
2. Percentage of schedule changes within near (firm zone) horizon
3. Performance vs. schedule in Finishing/Final Assembly per customer order, where appropriate
4. Linearity of output (by department and to finished goods and/or
   shipping)

MATERIAL PLANNING AND CONTROL

1. Inventory levels (by planner, by product line, by commodity type vs. seasonally adjusted targets, etc.)
2. Safety stock levels (by planner vs. seasonally adjusted targets, etc.)
3. Material availability (percentage of items available when needed, by week, by planner, by product line, etc.)
4. Planner action/exception messages (percentage of items vs. preestablished targets, percentage reviewed and acted upon, where appropriate, etc.)
5. Percentage of schedules/orders released with less than planned lead times (by planner, by product line, by supplier, by manufacturing department, etc.)
6. Percentage of schedules/orders rescheduled after release (by planner, by product line, by supplier, by department, etc.)
7. Unplanned activities (material substitutions, product design deviations, by planner, by product line, by department, etc.)

PRODUCTION PLANNING AND CONTROL

1. Percentage of schedules/orders completed on time (by work center/cell/line, by operation, by product line, etc.)
2. Percentage of schedules/orders received on time (by work center/cell/line, by operation, by product line, etc.)
3. Percentage of operations worked out of sequence (by department, work center/cell/line, etc.)
4. Percentage of schedules/orders split after initial release (by department, work center/cell/line, etc.)
5. Work-in-process levels (by work center/cell/line, in equivalent units and/or hours vs. seasonally adjusted targets, etc.)

PURCHASING

1. Percentage of delivery releases with full lead time
2. Percentage of changes to released delivery orders, firm schedules, etc.

CAPACITY PLANNING AND CONTROL

1. Demonstrated capacity (current levels, as compared to planned capacity, by work center/cell/line)
2. Input/output controls (actual input, where applicable, and output hours/units by work center/cell/line vs. targets)
3. Percentage of capacity plans past due (by work center/cell/line)
4. Percentage of schedules/orders routed to alternate work centers or subcontractors (by product line, by department or work center/cell/line)
5. Level of overtime work (by department, work center/cell/line vs. seasonally adjusted targets)
6. Work-in-process, manufacturing lead time, and queue levels (by work center/cell/line, in equivalent units and/or hours vs. seasonally adjusted targets, etc.)
7. Percentage of operations worked out of sequence (by department, work center/cell/line, etc.)
8. Percentage of schedules/orders split after initial release (by department, work center/cell/line, etc.)
9. Percentage of schedules/orders received on time (by work center/cell/line, by operation, by product line, etc.)

BILLS OF MATERIAL

1. Percent of sampled bills correct
2. Percent of item master records correct (includes planning parameters, descriptive data, etc., by planner, by product)
3. Bills of material change response time

INVENTORY RECORDS

1. Percent of inventory item/locations accurate
2. Percent of work orders accurate (includes checks on actual order quantity and work center location)

ROUTINGS

1. Percent of sampled routings correct
2. Routing change response time

DISTRIBUTION RESOURCE PLANNING

1. Distribution inventory turnover (by distribution center, by product)
2. Freight cost (from manufacturing to distribution centers, distribution center to distribution center transfers, total)

Appendix C
LIST OF OLIVER WIGHT PUBLICATIONS

The Oliver Wight ABCD Checklist For Operational Excellence
Inventory Record Accuracy
Manufacturing Data Structures
Master Scheduling
Gaining Control—Capacity Management & Scheduling
Manufacturing Resource Planning—MRP II
Distribution Resource Planning
MRP II: Making It Happen
Orchestrating Success
World-Class Production Inventory Management
Purchasing in the 21ˢᵗ Century
The Marketing Edge
MRP II Standard System
The Executive's Guide to Successful MRP II
JUST-IN-TIME: Making It Happen
The Right Choice